The Essence of Austr␣

Preparation Guide

Alexander Becker

TABLE OF CONTENTS

Introduction

Welcome to the land Down Under, where adventure meets natural beauty and vibrant cities captivate the senses. Australia, a country of vast landscapes and diverse ecosystems, is a dream destination for travelers seeking unforgettable experiences. From the stunning Great Barrier Reef to the iconic Sydney Opera House, this continent-sized country offers a wealth of treasures waiting to be explored.

Australia is a land of contrasts, where ancient Aboriginal culture intertwines with modern cosmopolitanism. Whether you're looking to bask in the sun-kissed beaches of the Gold Coast, immerse yourself in the rugged Outback, or wander through the bustling laneways of Melbourne, Australia beckons with its unique blend of urban sophistication and untamed wilderness.

One of the world's most biodiverse countries, Australia boasts an abundance of natural wonders that will leave you in awe. Marvel at the mystical beauty of Uluru (Ayers Rock), an imposing monolith rising from the heart of the red desert. Take a dip in the crystal-clear waters of the Whitsunday Islands or embark on a journey along the Great Ocean Road, where breathtaking cliffs meet the crashing waves of the Southern Ocean.

Venture beneath the surface and discover the extraordinary marine life of the Great Barrier Reef, a UNESCO World Heritage site teeming with vibrant coral reefs and exotic fish. For wildlife enthusiasts, encounters with kangaroos, koalas, and the elusive Tasmanian devil are just a small part of the unique fauna that call Australia home.

As you traverse the vastness of this captivating country, you'll also encounter a rich tapestry of cultures and cuisines. From indulging in fresh seafood in Sydney's harborside restaurants to savoring indigenous flavors in the heart of the Outback, Australia's culinary scene is as diverse as its landscapes.

In this travel guide, we'll take you on a journey through Australia's most iconic destinations, hidden gems, and insider tips. Whether you're planning a thrilling road trip along the legendary Great Ocean Road or seeking to immerse yourself in the bustling energy of Melbourne's vibrant arts scene, we've got you covered. So pack your sense of adventure, embrace the laid-back Aussie spirit, and get ready to discover the wonders of Australia, where extraordinary experiences await at every turn.

CHAPTER ONE

• *Welcome to Australia*

G'day mate! Welcome to the land Down Under, where adventure awaits at every turn. Australia, a vast and diverse country, is a destination like no other. From stunning coastlines to rugged outback landscapes, vibrant cities to ancient rainforests, Australia offers a wealth of experiences that will leave you awe-inspired. In this comprehensive travel guide, we'll take you on a journey across this remarkable continent, providing you with insights, tips, and recommendations to make the most of your time in Australia. So grab your sunscreen, put on your hiking boots, and let's embark on an unforgettable adventure!

Australia at a Glance:

Spanning an area of approximately 7.7 million square kilometers, Australia is the world's sixth-largest country. It is located in the southern hemisphere, surrounded by the Indian and Pacific Oceans. Australia is known for its unique wildlife, stunning landscapes, and multicultural cities. The country is divided into six states and two territories, each offering its own distinct attractions and experiences.

Climate and Best Time to Visit:
Australia's climate varies from tropical in the north to temperate in the south. Due to its size, different regions experience different weather patterns. Generally, the best time to visit is during the spring (September to November) and autumn (March to May) when temperatures are mild and rainfall is lower. However, specific regions like the Great Barrier Reef or the Red Centre may have different optimal seasons. It's essential to plan according to the activities and destinations you wish to explore.

Top Destinations:
a) Sydney: Start your Australian adventure in Sydney, the country's largest city and a global icon. Visit the Sydney Opera House, take a stroll across the iconic Sydney Harbour Bridge, and relax on the famous Bondi Beach. Explore the Royal Botanic Garden, climb the Sydney Tower for panoramic views, and indulge in the city's vibrant dining scene.

b) Melbourne: Head south to Melbourne, known for its artsy vibe, coffee culture, and sporting events. Discover hidden laneways adorned with street art, explore the trendy neighborhoods of Fitzroy and St. Kilda, and experience the city's renowned food scene. Don't miss visiting the Queen Victoria Market and catching a game of Australian Rules Football at the Melbourne Cricket Ground.

c) Great Barrier Reef: Dive into the world's largest coral reef system, a UNESCO World Heritage site. Snorkel or scuba dive amidst the colorful marine life, relax on picturesque islands like Hamilton Island, or take a scenic flight over the reef for a bird's-eye view. The Great Barrier Reef offers an enchanting underwater world that will leave you mesmerized.

d) Uluru-Kata Tjuta National Park: Journey to the Red Centre and witness the majestic Uluru (Ayers Rock). This sacred monolith is a spiritual site for the Aboriginal people and is best experienced during sunrise or sunset when the rock transforms into a mesmerizing palette of colors. Explore the nearby Kata Tjuta (the Olgas) for a glimpse of the region's geological wonders.

e) Great Ocean Road: Take a road trip along one of the world's most scenic coastal drives. The Great Ocean Road stretches for 243 kilometers, offering breathtaking views of rugged cliffs, pristine beaches, and the famous Twelve Apostles rock formations. Make stops at charming coastal towns like Lorne and Apollo Bay and immerse yourself in the beauty of this iconic route.

f) Tasmania: Escape to the island state of Tasmania, a nature lover's paradise. Explore the rugged landscapes of Cradle Mountain-Lake St. Clair National Park, wander through the historic streets of Hobart, and marvel at the unique wildlife in Freycinet National Park. Don't miss the chance to indulge in fresh seafood and local produce at the renowned Salamanca Market.

Outdoor Adventures:
Australia is a playground for outdoor enthusiasts, offering a myriad of adventure activities. From snorkeling in the Great Barrier Reef to surfing the world-class breaks in Byron Bay, there's something for everyone. Hike the stunning trails of the Blue Mountains, go kayaking in the Katherine Gorge, or embark on

a camping trip in the remote Kimberley region. With diverse landscapes ranging from rainforests to deserts, Australia provides endless opportunities for thrilling adventures.

Wildlife Encounters:

Australia is home to some of the world's most unique and fascinating wildlife. Explore Kangaroo Island, where you can spot sea lions, koalas, and kangaroos in their natural habitat. Visit Steve Irwin's Australia Zoo in Queensland to get up close with crocodiles, koalas, and a range of reptiles. For an unforgettable experience, witness the mesmerizing migration of humpback whales along the east coast or swim with whale sharks in Ningaloo Reef.

Indigenous Culture:

Discover the rich history and vibrant culture of Australia's Indigenous peoples. Visit ancient rock art sites in Kakadu National Park, learn about Dreamtime stories from local Aboriginal guides, and witness traditional dance performances. Immerse yourself in the world's oldest living culture and gain a deeper understanding of Australia's heritage.

Practical Tips:

a) Visa Requirements: Check the visa requirements for your country of origin before traveling to Australia. Apply well in advance to ensure a smooth entry into the country.

b) Health and Safety: Australia is generally a safe destination, but it's important to take precautions. Protect yourself from the sun, be mindful of wildlife encounters, and follow any safety instructions provided in national parks and coastal areas.

c) Transport: Australia has a well-developed transport system, including domestic flights, trains, buses, and rental cars. Plan your itinerary and choose the most convenient mode of transport for each leg of your journey.

d) Currency: The currency used in Australia is the Australian Dollar (AUD). Credit cards are widely accepted, but it's always handy to carry some cash, especially when visiting remote areas.

e) Respect Local Customs: Familiarize yourself with local customs and cultural sensitivities. Australians are known for their friendly and laid-back nature, so embrace the local way of life and enjoy the relaxed atmosphere.

Australia is a destination that promises adventure, natural beauty, and cultural richness. From iconic landmarks to hidden gems, this vast continent has something to offer every traveler. Whether you're seeking adrenaline-pumping experiences, tranquil beaches, or immersive cultural encounters, Australia delivers it all. So pack your bags, set out on an extraordinary journey, and create memories that will last a lifetime. Welcome to Australia – a land of wonders and boundless exploration!

•Quick Facts about Australia

Location: Australia is located in the Southern Hemisphere and is the largest country in Oceania. It is situated between the Indian and Pacific Oceans.

Capital City: Canberra is the capital city of Australia. However, Sydney is the largest city in the country and a major international hub.

Population: Australia has a population of approximately 26 million people. It is known for its multicultural society, with people from diverse backgrounds and ethnicities.

Language: English is the official language of Australia. However, due to its multicultural nature, many other languages are spoken in the country.

Government: Australia is a federal parliamentary constitutional monarchy. It has a parliamentary democracy with a constitutional monarch as the head of state. The current monarch is Queen Elizabeth II.

Indigenous People: Australia has a rich indigenous history dating back tens of thousands of years. The Aboriginal and Torres Strait Islander peoples are the original inhabitants of the country and have a unique cultural heritage.

Wildlife: Australia is renowned for its unique and diverse wildlife. It is home to various iconic species such as kangaroos, koalas, platypuses, and wombats. It is also known for its reptiles, including snakes and crocodiles.

Great Barrier Reef: The Great Barrier Reef, located off the northeastern coast of Australia, is the largest coral reef system in the world. It is a UNESCO World Heritage site and a popular tourist destination.

Landmarks: Australia has several famous landmarks, including the Sydney Opera House, Uluru (Ayers Rock), the Great Ocean Road, the Twelve Apostles, and the iconic Bondi Beach.

Sports: Australians are avid sports enthusiasts, and popular sports include cricket, Australian Rules football, rugby, soccer, tennis, and swimming. The country has a strong sporting culture and has achieved success in various international competitions.

CHAPTER TWO

Planning Your Trip

•*When to Visit*

Australia, the Land Down Under, is a vast and diverse country that offers a plethora of natural wonders, vibrant cities, unique wildlife, and a rich cultural heritage. When planning your trip to Australia, choosing the right time to visit is crucial to ensure you make the most of your experience. This travel guide will provide you with valuable insights into the different seasons, climates, and events throughout the year, helping you determine the best time to visit Australia based on your interests and preferences.

Summer (December to February):
Australia experiences summer during the months of December to February. This season is characterized by long, sunny days and warm temperatures. It is an ideal time to explore

Australia's stunning coastline, indulge in water sports, and witness the vibrant marine life at the Great Barrier Reef. However, it's important to note that popular tourist destinations can get crowded, and accommodation prices may be higher during this peak season.

Autumn (March to May):

Autumn in Australia, from March to May, offers pleasant temperatures and fewer crowds compared to the summer months. The weather is mild, making it an excellent time for outdoor activities such as hiking, wine tasting in the renowned vineyards of the Barossa Valley, or exploring the iconic national parks like the Blue Mountains or Uluru. Autumn is also the season for various cultural festivals and events, such as the Melbourne Food and Wine Festival or the Sydney Royal Easter Show.

Winter (June to August):

Winter in Australia, spanning from June to August, varies greatly depending on the region. Northern parts of Australia, such as Queensland and the Northern Territory, have milder temperatures, while the southern states experience cooler weather. This is the best time to explore the stunning landscapes of the Australian Alps for skiing or snowboarding enthusiasts. The winter months also offer the chance to witness breathtaking natural phenomena like whale migration along the east coast or experience unique events such as the Vivid Sydney Festival.

Spring (September to November):

Spring, from September to November, brings colorful blooms and a sense of renewal to Australia. This season offers mild temperatures and is particularly pleasant for exploring the outdoors, including visiting national parks, witnessing stunning wildflower displays in Western Australia, or experiencing the Great Ocean Road's scenic beauty. Spring is also a time when Australia hosts major sporting events like the Melbourne Cup horse race, attracting visitors from around the world.

Special Considerations:

a) School Holidays: If you are traveling with children or wish to avoid crowds, it is essential to be aware of Australian school holidays. These periods, particularly during summer and autumn, can significantly impact popular tourist destinations and availability of accommodations.

b) Climate Variations: Australia's diverse geography leads to significant climate variations across the country. While northern regions experience tropical climates, the southern areas can have more temperate or even alpine climates. Make sure to consider these variations and pack accordingly to ensure your comfort during your visit.

c) Regional Events: Australia hosts a wide array of regional events throughout the year, such as music festivals, sporting events, and cultural celebrations. Researching and aligning your visit with these events can provide unique experiences and insights into local culture.

• *Visa and Entry Requirements*

Australia is a fascinating country that offers diverse landscapes, unique wildlife, vibrant cities, and a rich cultural heritage. If you're planning a trip to Australia, it's essential to familiarize yourself with the visa and entry requirements to ensure a smooth and hassle-free travel experience. This comprehensive Australia travel guide will provide you with all the necessary information about visas, entry permits, and immigration procedures, helping you plan your trip with confidence.

Visa Types

Australia offers various visa types based on the purpose and duration of your visit. The most common visas for travelers include:

a) Visitor Visa (Subclass 600): This visa is suitable for tourists, family visits, or business purposes and allows you to stay in Australia for up to three, six, or twelve months, depending on the stream chosen.

b) Working Holiday Visa (Subclass 417/462): Intended for young travelers aged 18-30 (or 35 for select countries), this visa allows you to work and holiday in Australia for up to 12 or 24 months, depending on the visa subclass.

c) Student Visa (Subclass 500): If you plan to study in Australia for more than three months, you'll need a student visa. It permits you to stay for the duration of your course and may allow limited work rights.

d) Temporary Work Visa (Subclass 482): This visa enables skilled workers to work in Australia for up to four years, sponsored by an employer.

Electronic Travel Authority (ETA)

The Electronic Travel Authority (ETA) is an electronically stored authority for short-term visits to Australia. It is available for passport holders from eligible countries and allows multiple entries within a 12-month period for stays of up to three months per visit. The ETA can be obtained online, through travel agents, or airlines. The application process is straightforward, requiring passport details and a small fee.

eVisitor Visa

The eVisitor visa is similar to the ETA and is available to passport holders from certain European countries. It allows multiple entries within a 12-month period, with each stay up to three months. The eVisitor visa is free and can be applied for online.

Visa Application Process

To apply for a visa to Australia, you can submit an online application through the official Australian Government website or via paper applications if applicable. The process typically involves:

a) Completing the application form accurately with all required information.

b) Uploading the necessary documents, such as passport scans, photographs, and supporting documents (e.g., financial proof, health insurance, etc.).

c) Paying the visa application fee, which varies depending on the visa type and duration.

d) Waiting for the visa processing time, which can range from a few days to several weeks.

It's essential to apply for your visa well in advance of your intended travel date to avoid any last-minute complications.

Entry and Customs Procedures

When arriving in Australia, you'll need to go through immigration and customs procedures. Here are some key points to keep in mind:

a) Immigration Arrival Card: Upon arrival, you'll be required to complete an immigration arrival card with your personal details, purpose of visit, and customs declaration.

b) Customs and Quarantine: Australia has strict biosecurity regulations to protect its unique ecosystem. Declare any prohibited items such as food, plants, or animal products to avoid penalties.

c) Passenger Screening: Depending on your arrival point, you may undergo biosecurity screenings, baggage checks, and electronic passport scanning.

d) Visa Validation: Ensure that your visa is valid for the intended duration of your stay, as overstaying your visa may result in penalties or future visa complications.

Understanding Australia's visa and entry requirements is crucial for a smooth and enjoyable travel experience. This Australia travel guide has provided an overview of the various visa types, including visitor visas, working holiday visas, student visas, and temporary work visas. Additionally, it covered the Electronic Travel Authority (ETA) and eVisitor visa options, which are suitable for short-term visits.

Remember to carefully follow the visa application process, including completing the required forms, submitting supporting documents, and paying the necessary fees. Applying well in advance of your travel date will help ensure a timely approval.

Upon arrival in Australia, comply with immigration and customs procedures, including completing the immigration arrival card, adhering to biosecurity regulations, and respecting visa conditions.

It is advisable to check the official Australian Government website or consult with the nearest Australian embassy or consulate in your home country for the most up-to-date and accurate information regarding visa and entry requirements.

With this knowledge and proper preparation, you can embark on your Australian adventure with confidence, knowing you've met all the necessary visa and entry obligations. Enjoy your journey and explore all the wonders that Australia has to offer!

•Transportation

Australia, the land down under, is a vast and diverse country with breathtaking landscapes, vibrant cities, and unique wildlife. As you plan your trip to this beautiful continent, it is essential to understand the transportation options available to navigate the vast distances and explore the incredible destinations. This comprehensive Australia travel guide aims to provide you with insights into various modes of transportation, helping you make informed decisions and optimize your travel experience.

Air Travel:

Australia's expansive size makes air travel an efficient and popular choice for domestic travel. With a well-developed aviation network, major cities like Sydney, Melbourne, Brisbane, and Perth are well connected, offering frequent flights to regional centers and tourist destinations. Qantas, Virgin Australia, and Jetstar are among the major airlines operating domestic flights. It is advisable to book flights in advance to secure affordable fares and to check for any baggage restrictions or additional fees.

Rail Travel:

For those seeking a scenic and leisurely journey, Australia's rail network offers an excellent way to explore the country's diverse landscapes. The iconic Indian Pacific, The Ghan, and The Overland are renowned long-distance train journeys that connect major cities and showcase the stunning beauty of the outback. Additionally, suburban trains and light rail systems are available in major cities like Sydney, Melbourne, Brisbane, Adelaide, and Perth, providing convenient transportation within urban areas.

Road Travel:
Australia boasts a vast network of well-maintained roads, making road trips a popular choice for travelers. Renting a car or campervan offers the freedom to explore at your own pace and discover hidden gems along the way. However, it is essential to familiarize yourself with Australia's road rules, drive on the left-hand side of the road, and be aware of the long distances between destinations. Major highways like the Great Ocean Road, the Pacific Highway, and the Nullarbor Plain offer breathtaking coastal and outback drives.

Public Transportation:
Australia's major cities have efficient public transportation systems that provide convenient access to attractions, shopping districts, and cultural hotspots. Cities like Sydney, Melbourne, Brisbane, and Perth have extensive bus and train networks, as well as tram systems in some areas. Transport smartcards, such as the Opal card in Sydney and the myki card in

Melbourne, offer a convenient and cost-effective way to travel on public transport. These cards can be topped up and used across multiple modes of transportation.

Ferries and Water Transport:

Given Australia's vast coastline and numerous islands, ferries and water transport play a significant role in transportation. Sydney Harbour, for example, offers ferry services to popular destinations like Manly, Taronga Zoo, and Watsons Bay, providing a unique perspective of the city's iconic landmarks. Additionally, Queensland's Great Barrier Reef region and Tasmania's Bruny Island are among the many places where boat tours and cruises allow visitors to explore the stunning coastal and marine environments.

Cycling and Walking:

For those who enjoy an active and environmentally friendly mode of transportation, cycling and walking are great options. Many cities in Australia have well-established cycling paths, allowing visitors to explore urban areas and scenic routes. Melbourne, in particular, has an extensive bike-sharing program, making it easy to rent bicycles for short trips. Additionally, national parks and nature reserves offer a myriad of walking trails, allowing you to immerse yourself in Australia's natural beauty.

As you embark on your Australian adventure, understanding the transportation options available will greatly enhance your travel experience. From air travel for covering vast distances to scenic rail journeys and the freedom of road trips, Australia offers diverse modes of transportation to suit every traveler's preferences. Additionally, public transportation, water transport, cycling, and walking provide convenient and eco-friendly alternatives. By utilizing this comprehensive Australia travel guide, you can navigate the vast continent with ease, ensuring a memorable and enjoyable journey.

Getting to Australia

Australia, with its diverse landscapes, stunning natural beauty, and unique wildlife, is a dream destination for many travelers. Getting to Australia might seem like a daunting task due to its geographical isolation, but with an extensive transportation network, reaching the Land Down Under is easier than you might think. In this travel guide, we will explore various transportation options available to reach Australia, including international flights, cruise ships, and other regional transportation methods.

I. International Flights:

A. Major Airports:

Sydney Airport (SYD)
Melbourne Airport (MEL)
Brisbane Airport (BNE)
Perth Airport (PER)
Adelaide Airport (ADL)
Cairns Airport (CNS)
B. Airlines:

Qantas Airways
Virgin Australia
Emirates
Singapore Airlines
Cathay Pacific
Etihad Airways
C. Connecting Flights:

Transfers through Asia: Hong Kong, Singapore, Kuala Lumpur, Dubai
Transfers through the Americas: Los Angeles, San Francisco, Vancouver
Transfers through Europe: London, Paris, Frankfurt, Amsterdam

II. *Cruise Ships:*
A. Ports of Call:

Sydney Harbor
Melbourne
Brisbane
Fremantle
Cairns
Adelaide
B. Cruise Lines:

Royal Caribbean International
Princess Cruises
Carnival Cruise Line
P&O Cruises Australia
Celebrity Cruises
C. Itineraries:

Pacific cruises from the United States or Canada
Asian cruises from Singapore or Hong Kong
Transpacific cruises from Europe

III. Regional Transportation:
A. Domestic Flights:

Qantas Airways
Virgin Australia
Jetstar Airways
Regional Express Airlines (REX)
Tigerair Australia
B. Trains:

The Indian Pacific: Sydney to Perth
The Ghan: Adelaide to Darwin
The Overland: Melbourne to Adelaide
The Spirit of Queensland: Brisbane to Cairns
C. Buses:

Greyhound Australia
Premier Motor Service
Firefly Express

IV. Visa and Entry Requirements:
A. Electronic Travel Authority (ETA)
B. Visitor Visa (subclass 600)
C. Working Holiday Visa (subclass 417)

Reaching Australia is an exciting journey, and with various transportation options available, it can be tailored to suit individual preferences and budgets. Whether you choose to fly into one of Australia's major airports, embark on a cruise ship adventure, or explore the country through regional transportation, Australia offers an unforgettable experience to every traveler. So, pack your bags, plan your itinerary, and get ready to embark on a remarkable adventure in the Land Down Under.

Getting Around within Australia

Australia, known for its stunning landscapes, diverse wildlife, and vibrant cities, offers a plethora of attractions for travelers. To fully experience the wonders of this vast continent, it's crucial to understand the various transportation options available. This comprehensive guide will explore the different modes of transport within Australia, highlighting their advantages, costs, and suitability for different travel preferences.

Air Travel:

Australia boasts an extensive domestic air network, making it an efficient and time-saving option for long-distance travel. Major airlines such as Qantas, Virgin Australia, and Jetstar operate flights between major cities, regional towns, and popular tourist destinations. Domestic flights are well-regulated and offer comfort, convenience, and competitive fares. Booking in advance and comparing prices can often lead to significant savings. Additionally, frequent flyer programs and airline alliances provide opportunities to accumulate points for future travel benefits.

Rail Travel:

For those seeking a more scenic and leisurely journey, rail travel in Australia offers unique experiences. The iconic Indian Pacific, Ghan, and Overland trains traverse vast distances, allowing travelers to witness the country's diverse landscapes in style. The Indian Pacific connects Sydney and Perth, offering a breathtaking transcontinental journey. The Ghan takes passengers from Adelaide to Darwin, showcasing the majestic Outback scenery. The Overland connects Melbourne and Adelaide, providing a picturesque coastal and rural experience. Rail travel not only offers comfortable accommodations but also dining cars and observation decks to fully appreciate the beauty of Australia's countryside.

Road Travel:

Australia's expansive road network makes road trips a popular choice for travelers. Renting a car or campervan provides the freedom to explore remote areas, hidden gems, and scenic routes at your own pace. The country has well-maintained highways, including the famous Great Ocean Road in Victoria, the Pacific Coast Drive in New South Wales, and the Nullarbor Plain crossing between South Australia and Western Australia. However, it's essential to familiarize yourself with local road rules, drive safely, and plan for long stretches between service stations in remote areas. Many car rental companies offer competitive rates, and advance bookings are advisable during peak travel seasons.

Bus and Coach Travel:

An economical and convenient option for getting around Australia is bus and coach travel. Several companies, such as Greyhound

Australia and Premier Motor Service, operate extensive networks connecting major cities, regional centers, and popular tourist destinations. These services offer flexibility, affordable fares, and various ticket options, including hop-on-hop-off passes. While bus travel might take longer than flying, it allows travelers to experience the country's diverse landscapes up close and meet fellow adventurers along the way.

Ferry Travel:

Australia's extensive coastline and numerous islands provide ample opportunities for ferry travel. Sydney Harbor, for instance, offers regular ferry services to popular destinations like Manly, Watsons Bay, and Taronga Zoo. Tasmania's Spirit of Tasmania ferry connects Melbourne with Devonport, providing a convenient transport option for travelers wishing to explore the island state. Ferry travel is a scenic and enjoyable way to appreciate Australia's coastal beauty, offering stunning views and the possibility of spotting marine wildlife.

Public Transportation:

Major cities in Australia, including Sydney, Melbourne, Brisbane, and Perth, have well-developed public transportation systems comprising trains, trams, buses, and ferries. These networks offer a cost-effective and efficient means of exploring urban areas, with various ticketing options available. For example, in Sydney, the Opal card allows seamless travel on trains, buses, and ferries, with fare discounts for multiple trips. Familiarize yourself with the public transport options in each city, as they can vary in terms of ticketing systems and coverage.

Navigating Australia's vast expanse is made easy with a range of transportation options catering to different travel preferences. Whether you prefer the speed and convenience of air travel, the scenic journeys by rail, the freedom of road trips, the affordability of bus travel, or the charm of ferry rides, Australia has it all. By utilizing this travel guide, you can plan your itinerary accordingly, maximizing your time and enjoyment as you explore the remarkable wonders of the Land Down Under.

•Currency and Money Matters

Traveling to Australia is an exciting adventure filled with diverse landscapes, unique wildlife, and vibrant cities. As you plan your trip, it's crucial to understand the currency and money matters in Australia to ensure a smooth and hassle-free experience. This comprehensive travel guide aims to provide you with essential information about Australian currency, banking, exchange rates, payment methods, and tips for managing your money effectively throughout your journey.

Australian Currency Overview:

Australia's official currency is the Australian Dollar (AUD), and it is recognized by the symbol "$" or "A$." The Australian Dollar is subdivided into 100 cents, with coins available in denominations of 5, 10, 20, and 50 cents, as well as $1 and $2 coins. Banknotes are issued in denominations of $5, $10, $20, $50, and $100. Familiarize yourself with the appearance and security features of Australian banknotes to avoid counterfeit currency.

Currency Exchange:

a. Preparing for Your Trip:
Before departing for Australia, it's advisable to exchange a small amount of your home

currency into Australian Dollars to cover immediate expenses upon arrival. You can do this at your local bank or currency exchange service.

b. Exchange Options in Australia:
Once you arrive in Australia, you'll find several options for currency exchange. Airports, major hotels, banks, and dedicated currency exchange offices are common places to convert your money. Compare exchange rates and fees to ensure you get the best value for your currency. It's worth noting that currency exchange services often charge a commission or fee for their services.

Banking and ATMs:
a. Banking Services:
Australia has a reliable and efficient banking system. Major banks such as Commonwealth Bank, ANZ, Westpac, and NAB offer a wide range of services, including currency exchange, international money transfers, and ATMs.

b. ATMs (Automatic Teller Machines):
ATMs are widely available throughout Australia, allowing you to withdraw cash in Australian Dollars using your debit or credit card. Keep in mind that your home bank may

charge international transaction fees or ATM withdrawal fees, so it's advisable to check with your bank before traveling. Additionally, notify your bank of your travel plans to prevent your card from being blocked for suspicious activity.

Payment Methods:
a. Cash Usage:
While cash is widely accepted in Australia, card payments are becoming increasingly popular. It's recommended to carry a small amount of cash for situations where card payments may not be accepted, such as smaller establishments or local markets.

b. Card Payments:
Credit and debit cards, especially Visa and Mastercard, are widely accepted across Australia. However, it's advisable to carry a backup card in case of any issues. Contactless payments, known as "tap and go," are also prevalent in Australia, making transactions quick and convenient.

c. Currency Conversion Fees:
Some credit cards charge currency conversion fees for transactions made in a foreign currency. Look for cards that offer low or no foreign transaction fees to minimize costs.

Budgeting and Cost of Living:

a. Cost of Accommodation:

Accommodation costs in Australia vary depending on location, season, and the type of lodging. Major cities like Sydney and Melbourne tend to have higher accommodation prices, while more budget-friendly options can be found in smaller towns and rural areas. Consider booking accommodation in advance to secure the best deals.

b. Transportation Expenses:

Australia has an extensive transportation network, including domestic flights, trains, buses, and ferries. Research and plan your transportation options according to your budget and itinerary. Public transportation, such as trains and buses, is generally affordable, while domestic flights can vary in price depending on the distance and season.

c. Dining and Entertainment:

Eating out in Australia can range from budget-friendly options to high-end dining experiences. It's advisable to explore local eateries and cafes to get a taste of Australian cuisine while saving money. Additionally, consider exploring free or low-cost attractions, parks, and cultural events to balance your entertainment expenses.

Understanding the currency and money matters in Australia is essential for a successful and enjoyable trip. Familiarize yourself with the Australian Dollar, exchange options, banking services, payment methods, and budgeting tips to make the most of your travel experience. By being prepared and informed, you can navigate Australia's financial landscape with ease and focus on immersing yourself in the country's rich culture, stunning landscapes, and memorable experiences.

•Language and Communication

Australia is a vibrant and diverse country, known for its stunning landscapes, unique wildlife, and rich cultural heritage. As a traveler exploring the vast continent, it's essential to understand the language and communication nuances that shape the Australian experience.

In this comprehensive travel guide, we will delve into the languages spoken in Australia, the country's unique dialects and accents, as well as cultural aspects of communication. Whether you're planning a visit to the bustling cities, remote outback regions, or picturesque coastal areas, this guide will equip you with the necessary knowledge to navigate and engage with locals effectively.

Languages Spoken in Australia

Australia is a linguistically diverse nation with over 200 languages spoken by its multicultural population. English, however, is the de facto national language and the primary means of communication throughout the country. Indigenous Australian languages hold significant historical and cultural value, with around 120 Indigenous languages still spoken to varying degrees. These languages are an integral part of Aboriginal and Torres Strait Islander cultures, reflecting the deep connection between the people and the land.

Australian English: Dialects and Accents

While English is the dominant language, Australian English has developed its own unique characteristics, including distinct dialects and accents. The Australian accent is often characterized by its relaxed and melodic nature, influenced by the country's diverse linguistic heritage. Variations in pronunciation, vocabulary, and idiomatic expressions can be found across different regions. From the "ocker" accent of the working-class to the more cosmopolitan speech of urban areas, understanding these nuances can enhance your interactions with locals and immerse you in the authentic Australian experience.

Non-Verbal Communication

Non-verbal communication plays a crucial role in Australia, and understanding the cultural context is essential for effective interaction. Australians value personal space, and it is common to maintain a comfortable physical distance during conversations. Eye contact is generally expected and seen as a sign of attentiveness and respect. Hand gestures are widely used to emphasize points, but it's important to avoid offensive or aggressive gestures, as they may be misinterpreted. A warm smile and a friendly demeanor can go a long way in establishing rapport and creating positive connections with locals.

Slang and Colloquialisms

Australian English is renowned for its colorful slang and colloquialisms, which can often confuse international travelers. Phrases like "G'day," "mate," and "no worries" are commonly used and reflect the country's laid-back and friendly culture. Embracing and understanding this unique vocabulary can enhance your interactions, as locals appreciate the effort made to connect on a more familiar level. However, it's important to be mindful of the context and avoid using slang that may be considered offensive or inappropriate.

Cultural Sensitivity and Etiquette

Respecting and understanding Australian cultural sensitivities is crucial as a traveler. Australia is a culturally diverse nation that values inclusivity and tolerance. Acknowledging and showing respect for Aboriginal and Torres Strait Islander cultures, traditions, and customs is important. Additionally, being aware of the country's colonial history and its impact on Indigenous communities can foster meaningful and respectful interactions. It's also essential to be conscious of cultural norms such as punctuality, respecting personal boundaries, and adhering to local customs when visiting sacred sites or participating in cultural events.

Language and communication are vital aspects of any travel experience, and Australia is no exception. By gaining an understanding of the languages spoken, the unique characteristics of Australian English, non-verbal communication cues, slang and colloquialisms, and cultural sensitivities, you can enhance your interactions, forge connections with locals

•Travel Insurance

Traveling to Australia is an exciting experience, but like any adventure, it comes with its share of uncertainties. To mitigate the risks associated with traveling, it is essential to have adequate travel insurance coverage. In this comprehensive Australia travel insurance guide, we will explore the importance of travel insurance, the types of coverage available, key considerations for choosing a policy, and some of the best insurance providers in Australia.

Understanding the Importance of Travel Insurance:

1.1 Protection against medical emergencies: Australia offers excellent healthcare facilities, but medical expenses can be exorbitant, especially for travelers without insurance.

1.2 Trip cancellation or interruption coverage: Travel insurance safeguards your investment by reimbursing non-refundable costs in case of unexpected trip cancellations or interruptions.

1.3 Lost or delayed baggage coverage: Baggage mishaps are not uncommon during travel, and travel insurance can provide compensation for lost or delayed baggage.

1.4 Emergency evacuation and repatriation: In the event of a medical emergency or natural disaster, travel insurance covers the cost of emergency evacuation and repatriation.

1.5 Personal liability coverage: Travel insurance protects you from potential legal and financial liabilities arising from accidental damage or injury to others.

Types of Travel Insurance Coverage:

2.1 Medical coverage: This covers medical expenses, hospitalization, emergency medical evacuation, and repatriation of remains.

2.2 Trip cancellation and interruption coverage: Reimbursement for non-refundable expenses due to unexpected events like illness, injury, natural disasters, or other covered reasons.

2.3 Baggage and personal belongings coverage: Compensation for lost, stolen, or damaged baggage, as well as reimbursement for essential items in case of baggage delay.

2.4 Personal liability coverage: Protection against legal expenses and compensation for damages caused to others due to accidental injury or property damage.

2.5 Travel delay coverage: Reimbursement for additional expenses incurred due to delayed departures, missed connections, or other travel disruptions.

2.6 Emergency assistance services: Access to 24/7 emergency assistance for travel-related issues such as lost documents, medical referrals, or travel advisories.

Key Considerations for Choosing a Travel Insurance Policy:

3.1 Coverage limits and exclusions: Understand the maximum limits for each coverage type and review the policy's exclusions to ensure it meets your specific needs.

3.2 Pre-existing medical conditions: Declare any pre-existing medical conditions to ensure they are covered, or consider purchasing a policy with a pre-existing condition waiver if eligible.

3.3 Duration and frequency of travel: Determine if you need a single trip or annual multi-trip policy based on the number and duration of your trips to Australia.

3.4 Activities and sports coverage: If you plan to engage in adventure sports or other high-risk activities, confirm that your policy includes coverage for such activities.

3.5 Policy cost: Compare quotes from different insurance providers to find the best balance between coverage and affordability.

3.6 Customer reviews and reputation: Research the insurer's reputation for customer service, claims handling, and financial stability.

Prominent Travel Insurance Providers in Australia:

4.1 Allianz Global Assistance: Known for their comprehensive coverage options and reliable customer service.

4.2 Cover-More: Offers a range of policies with various coverage levels, including optional add-ons for adventure sports and rental vehicle excess.

4.3 World Nomads: Popular among backpackers and adventure travelers, providing coverage for a wide range of adventure activities.

4.4 SCTI (Southern Cross Travel Insurance): Offers competitive prices and flexible policies with options for pre-existing conditions and senior travelers.

4.5 QBE Insurance: A reputable insurer with extensive coverage options and additional benefits like concierge services and travel safety advice.

Travel insurance is an essential component of planning any trip to Australia. It provides financial protection and peace of mind, ensuring you can fully enjoy your journey without worrying about unexpected expenses or mishaps. By understanding the importance of travel insurance, the various coverage options available, and key considerations for selecting a policy, you can make an informed decision and choose the best travel insurance provider in Australia. Safeguard your trip and explore the wonders of Australia with confidence, knowing you have comprehensive travel insurance coverage.

• *Safety and Health Tips*

Traveling to Australia can be an incredible experience, offering breathtaking landscapes, unique wildlife, vibrant cities, and a rich cultural heritage. While exploring this vast and diverse country, it is crucial to prioritize your safety and well-being. This comprehensive Australia travel guide provides essential safety and health tips to ensure a memorable and trouble-free journey.

I. Pre-Trip Planning:

Research and Familiarize Yourself with the Destination:

Gain knowledge about the regions you plan to visit, including their weather patterns, local customs, and any potential safety concerns.

Stay updated on travel advisories and government warnings for the areas you intend to explore.

Travel Insurance:

Obtain comprehensive travel insurance that covers medical emergencies, trip cancellation or interruption, lost or stolen belongings, and personal liability. Ensure your insurance policy covers any adventure activities or outdoor pursuits you plan to undertake.

II. Health Tips:

Vaccinations and Medications:

Consult your healthcare provider well in advance to determine if you require any vaccinations or prophylactic medications based on your destination and personal health history.

Carry a sufficient supply of any prescription medications you regularly take, along with copies of your prescriptions.

Sun Protection:

Australia's high UV levels necessitate adequate sun protection measures.

Use broad-spectrum sunscreen (SPF 30+), wear a wide-brimmed hat, sunglasses, and lightweight, long-sleeved clothing.

Seek shade during the hottest part of the day (11 am - 3 pm).

Hydration and Food Safety:

Stay hydrated by drinking plenty of water, especially in hot and arid areas.

Consume safe, clean drinking water, and avoid drinking from untreated water sources.

Practice good food hygiene, such as washing hands before eating, consuming thoroughly cooked food, and avoiding street food with questionable sanitation practices.

Insect Protection:

Australia is home to various insects that can pose health risks.

Use insect repellents containing DEET, picaridin, or oil of lemon eucalyptus to protect against mosquitoes and other biting insects.

Consider using bed nets or screens in areas where insects are prevalent, especially in tropical regions.

III. Safety Tips:

Personal Safety:

Be vigilant and aware of your surroundings, particularly in crowded tourist areas and public transport.

Keep your belongings secure and avoid displaying valuable items openly.

Use reputable transportation services and be cautious while using ridesharing apps.

Outdoor Activities and Wildlife Encounters:

Follow safety guidelines and regulations while engaging in adventure activities such as hiking, snorkeling, or diving.

Respect wildlife and maintain a safe distance, especially when encountering animals in their natural habitats.

Stay informed about potential hazards, such as venomous snakes and jellyfish, in specific regions and take necessary precautions.

Water Safety:

Observe warning signs and swim only in designated areas with lifeguards present.

Be cautious of strong currents, riptides, and changing tidal conditions when swimming in coastal areas.

Familiarize yourself with local surf conditions if planning to engage in water sports.

Road Safety:

> Observe local traffic laws and regulations, including speed limits and seatbelt usage.
>
> If driving, adjust to driving on the left side of the road and familiarize yourself with local road rules.
>
> Take regular breaks during long journeys and avoid driving while fatigued.

IV. Emergency Preparedness:

Emergency Contact Information:

> Save emergency contact numbers, including local authorities, your country's embassy or consulate, and your travel insurance provider, on your phone or in a readily accessible location.

First Aid Kit:

> Carry a basic first aid kit containing essentials such as band-aids, antiseptic cream, pain relievers, and any personal medications.

Communication and Navigation:

> Ensure you have a working mobile phone and charger with you at all times.

Download offline maps or utilize GPS navigation apps to help you navigate unfamiliar areas.

By prioritizing safety and health while exploring Australia, you can make the most of your journey without compromising your well-being. Remember to plan ahead, stay informed, and take necessary precautions. By adhering to the tips provided in this Australia travel guide, you can have a memorable and worry-free experience as you immerse yourself in the wonders of this extraordinary country.

CHAPTER THREE

Sydney

•*Overview of Sydney*

Sydney, the capital city of New South Wales, is one of Australia's most vibrant and iconic destinations. With its stunning harbor, beautiful beaches, world-class attractions, and diverse cultural scene, Sydney offers a wealth of experiences for travelers. Whether you're a nature lover, a history buff, a foodie, or an adventure seeker, Sydney has something for everyone. In this Australia travel guide, we will explore the highlights of Sydney and provide you with essential information to make the most of your visit.

Geography and Climate:

Sydney is situated on the southeastern coast of Australia, stretching along the Tasman Sea. The city is built around the iconic Sydney Harbour, which is renowned for its natural beauty and is home to famous landmarks such as the Sydney Opera House and the Sydney Harbour Bridge. The metropolitan area of

Sydney covers an extensive area, with suburbs spreading out in all directions.

Sydney enjoys a temperate climate, with mild winters and warm summers. The average temperature in summer (December to February) ranges from 20 to 26 degrees Celsius (68 to 79 degrees Fahrenheit), while in winter (June to August), temperatures typically range from 8 to 17 degrees Celsius (46 to 63 degrees Fahrenheit). Rainfall is spread fairly evenly throughout the year, although spring and summer tend to be slightly wetter.

Transportation:

Sydney has a well-developed transportation system that makes getting around the city and its surrounding areas relatively easy. The city's main airport, Sydney Airport (Kingsford Smith), is located just a short distance from the city center and serves both domestic and international flights. From the airport, you can reach the city by train, bus, taxi, or rideshare services.

Within the city, Sydney's public transportation network consists of trains, buses, ferries, and light rail. The train system is extensive and connects various suburbs and neighboring cities. Buses are a convenient way to travel within the city and reach destinations not serviced by trains. Ferries offer a scenic way to explore Sydney Harbour and visit popular waterfront attractions. The light rail network primarily serves the inner-western suburbs of the city.

Attractions and Landmarks:

Sydney is renowned for its iconic landmarks that have become synonymous with the city's identity. The Sydney Opera House is perhaps the most famous of these landmarks, with its distinctive sail-like architecture. Guided tours are available to explore the interior of this architectural masterpiece or you can catch a performance at one of the Opera House's many venues.

Adjacent to the Opera House, the Sydney Harbour Bridge stands tall, offering panoramic views of the city. For the adventurous, the BridgeClimb experience allows visitors to climb to the summit of the bridge and enjoy breathtaking vistas. Alternatively, you can stroll across the pedestrian walkway or take a harbor cruise to admire the bridge from below.

Bondi Beach, located in Sydney's eastern suburbs, is a popular destination for both locals and tourists. With its golden sands, rolling surf, and vibrant beach culture, Bondi offers a quintessential Australian beach experience. The beach is lined with trendy cafes, restaurants, and boutiques, making it a perfect spot to relax, people-watch, or catch a wave.

For nature lovers, a visit to the Royal Botanic Garden is a must. Located in the heart of the city, this lush oasis showcases a diverse range of plants and flowers, as well as stunning views of the harbor. You can take a leisurely stroll through the gardens, join a guided tour, or have a picnic on the lawns.

If you're interested in history and culture, Sydney offers several museums and cultural institutions worth exploring. The Australian Museum provides insights into the country's natural history and indigenous cultures, while the Art Gallery of New South Wales houses an impressive collection of Australian and international artworks. The Museum of Contemporary Art features contemporary exhibitions and installations, showcasing the works of both local and international artists.

Cuisine and Dining:

Sydney is a melting pot of cultures, and its dining scene reflects this diversity. From fine dining establishments to casual eateries and vibrant street food markets, there's something to suit every taste and budget. The city is particularly known for its fresh seafood, with fish markets offering a wide array of delicious ocean delicacies.

For a truly unique experience, head to the vibrant neighborhoods of Chinatown or Haymarket, where you can savor authentic Asian cuisine. The Rocks, a historic area near Sydney Harbour, is home to charming pubs, restaurants, and cafes where you can enjoy a meal while soaking up the area's colonial charm.

Events and Festivals:

Sydney hosts a variety of events and festivals throughout the year, adding to its vibrant atmosphere. One of the most famous events is the Sydney New Year's Eve fireworks display, which takes place over Sydney Harbour and attracts millions of spectators from around the world. The Vivid Sydney festival, held annually in winter, transforms the city into a mesmerizing outdoor gallery of light installations, music, and ideas.

In January, the city comes alive with the Sydney Festival, a three-week celebration of arts, culture, and entertainment. The Royal Easter Show, held in March or April, is a beloved tradition featuring agricultural displays, thrilling rides, and live entertainment. These are just a few examples of the many events that take place in Sydney, ensuring there's always something exciting happening.

Sydney's stunning natural beauty, rich history, and vibrant culture make it an ideal destination for travelers seeking a diverse and unforgettable experience. Whether you're exploring the iconic landmarks, lazing on beautiful beaches, indulging in delicious cuisine, or immersing yourself in the city's lively events, Sydney is sure to leave a lasting impression. So pack your bags, grab your camera, and get ready to discover the magic of Sydney, Australia's dynamic and captivating metropolis.

Top Attractions

Sydney, the bustling capital of New South Wales, Australia, is a vibrant and captivating city that seamlessly blends stunning natural beauty with a cosmopolitan lifestyle. From its iconic landmarks to its lively culture, Sydney offers an array of attractions that cater to every traveler's taste. In this comprehensive Australia travel guide, we will delve into the top attractions of Sydney, providing you with an immersive experience of this captivating city.

Sydney Opera House:

No visit to Sydney is complete without marveling at the Sydney Opera House. A UNESCO World Heritage Site, this architectural masterpiece is an iconic symbol of the city. Designed by Danish architect Jørn Utzon, the Opera House features a distinctive sail-like design and hosts a range of performances, including opera, ballet, and theater. Visitors can take guided tours to explore its interior or enjoy a performance in one of its stunning venues.

Sydney Harbour Bridge:

Dominating the city's skyline, the Sydney Harbour Bridge is another iconic landmark not to be missed. Known as the "Coathanger" by locals, this engineering marvel offers breathtaking views of the city and its harbor. Adventurous travelers can embark on a BridgeClimb, ascending the arches of the bridge for an exhilarating experience. Alternatively, a leisurely stroll along the pedestrian walkway provides a picturesque vantage point of the harbor and Opera House.

Bondi Beach:

Located just a few kilometers from the city center, Bondi Beach is a world-renowned destination for sun, sand, and surf. With its golden sands and turquoise waters, Bondi offers the perfect setting for beach lovers and water enthusiasts. Take a refreshing dip, learn to surf with experienced instructors, or simply relax and soak up the vibrant beach culture. The beach is also surrounded by trendy cafes, restaurants, and boutique shops, making it an ideal spot for a leisurely day out.

The Rocks:

Steeped in history and charm, The Rocks is Sydney's oldest neighborhood and a captivating blend of cobblestone streets, historic buildings, and vibrant markets. Explore its narrow laneways to discover art galleries, boutique shops, and traditional pubs. The Rocks Market, held every weekend, offers a delightful assortment of local crafts, fashion, and gourmet treats. Don't forget to visit the Museum of Contemporary Art, showcasing a diverse collection of modern art.

Taronga Zoo:

For an unforgettable wildlife experience, Taronga Zoo is a must-visit attraction. Located on the shores of Sydney Harbour, the zoo is home to a vast array of native and exotic animals. Explore the zoo's extensive grounds, which are beautifully landscaped and provide stunning views of the city skyline. Attend daily animal shows, get up close and personal with kangaroos and koalas, or embark on the Wild

Ropes adventure course for an adrenaline-filled experience.

Royal Botanic Garden:

Escape the urban hustle and immerse yourself in the tranquility of the Royal Botanic Garden. Situated near the Sydney Opera House, this magnificent garden offers a serene retreat with its lush landscapes, stunning plant collections, and picturesque harbor views. Take a leisurely stroll along the winding pathways, explore themed gardens, or enjoy a picnic in the shade of ancient trees. The garden also hosts various events and exhibitions throughout the year.

Darling Harbour:

A vibrant waterfront precinct, Darling Harbour is a hub of entertainment, dining, and attractions. Visit the SEA LIFE Sydney Aquarium to marvel at marine life from around the world, including sharks, penguins, and tropical fish. Immerse yourself in the interactive exhibits at the Australian National Maritime Museum, or enjoy the thrill of virtual reality at the 9D Action Cinema. Darling Harbour also boasts a wide range of restaurants, bars, and cafes, offering diverse culinary experiences.

Art Gallery of New South Wales:

Art enthusiasts will find solace in the Art Gallery of New South Wales. With an extensive collection of Australian, Asian, and European art, the gallery showcases masterpieces spanning various artistic periods. Discover works by renowned artists such as Sidney Nolan, Brett Whiteley, and Emily Kame Kngwarreye. The gallery also hosts temporary exhibitions, workshops, and guided tours, providing an enriching cultural experience for visitors.

Blue Mountains:

Just a short drive from Sydney, the Blue Mountains offer a breathtaking escape into nature's wonders. Explore the UNESCO World Heritage-listed national park, renowned for its dramatic cliffs, deep valleys, and cascading waterfalls. Witness the mesmerizing Three Sisters rock formation, take a scenic ride on the Katoomba Scenic Railway, or hike through enchanting bushland. The Blue Mountains provide countless opportunities for outdoor activities, including bushwalking, rock climbing, and abseiling.

Manly Beach:

Nestled on a picturesque peninsula, Manly Beach offers a laid-back coastal experience away from the city's hustle. Accessible by a scenic ferry ride, Manly boasts golden beaches, crystal-clear waters, and a vibrant seaside atmosphere. Stroll along the Corso, a bustling pedestrian mall lined with shops and cafes, or enjoy a leisurely bike ride along the waterfront promenade. For nature lovers, explore the nearby North Head, a haven for wildlife and panoramic views of Sydney Harbour.

Sydney, with its captivating blend of natural beauty, iconic landmarks, and vibrant culture, offers an unforgettable experience for travelers. From the architectural marvels of the Sydney Opera House and Harbour Bridge to the sun-soaked beaches of Bondi and Manly, the city presents a diverse range of attractions. Immerse yourself in history at The Rocks, explore wildlife at Taronga Zoo, or unwind in the serene Royal Botanic Garden. With its abundant offerings, Sydney truly stands as a remarkable destination within Australia's travel landscape.

Sydney Opera House

Australia is renowned for its diverse and breathtaking landscapes, vibrant cities, and rich cultural heritage. Among its many treasures, the Sydney Opera House stands as a proud symbol of the nation's artistic and architectural prowess. Located in the heart of Sydney, this iconic structure is a testament to human ingenuity and creative vision. In this Australia travel guide, we will explore the history, design, significance, and attractions of the Sydney Opera House, inviting you to immerse yourself in its captivating beauty and discover why it has become a must-visit destination for travelers from around the world.

Historical Background

The Sydney Opera House's story begins in the mid-20th century when the need for a grand performing arts venue in Sydney was recognized. In 1956, an international design competition was launched, attracting 233 entries from architects worldwide. Danish architect Jørn Utzon emerged victorious with his groundbreaking design featuring sail-like shells and a stunning waterfront location. Construction began in 1959, and after numerous challenges, the Sydney Opera House was officially opened by Queen Elizabeth II on October 20, 1973.

Architectural Marvel

The Sydney Opera House's architecture is nothing short of extraordinary. Its design embodies the fusion of art, engineering, and nature. The structure consists of a series of precast concrete shells that interlock to form the iconic sail-like rooflines. The building's unique shape and white ceramic tiles create a striking contrast against the backdrop of Sydney Harbor. The design allows for natural light to filter through the expansive glass walls, providing stunning views of the surrounding landscape. The attention to detail and innovative engineering techniques make the Sydney Opera House an architectural masterpiece.

Cultural Significance

Beyond its stunning aesthetics, the Sydney Opera House holds immense cultural significance for Australians and the global community. It serves as a vibrant hub for performing arts, hosting a diverse range of events, including opera, ballet, theater, music concerts, and festivals. The venue has showcased world-renowned artists and performers, attracting millions of visitors each year. Its inclusion in the UNESCO World Heritage list in 2007 further solidifies its status as a cultural gem of global importance.

Attractions and Experiences

Visiting the Sydney Opera House offers a plethora of attractions and experiences that cater to all interests. Guided tours provide an opportunity to explore the interior of the building, offering insights into its history, architecture, and behind-the-scenes operations. The Opera House's numerous performance spaces, including the Concert Hall, Opera Theatre, Drama Theatre, and Playhouse, offer an array of world-class productions throughout the year. From grand opera performances to contemporary theater productions, there is something for everyone.

For those seeking a more immersive experience, attending a live performance at the Sydney Opera House is an absolute must. The acoustics and atmosphere of the Concert Hall are renowned worldwide, ensuring a truly memorable experience. Additionally, the Opera House hosts free outdoor concerts, cultural festivals, and community events, providing a vibrant atmosphere for locals and tourists alike.

Surrounding Area and Amenities

Situated on Bennelong Point, the Sydney Opera House offers stunning views of Sydney Harbor, the Sydney Harbour Bridge, and the city skyline. Visitors can enjoy leisurely walks along the harbor promenade, capturing postcard-worthy photos of this iconic landmark. The Opera Bar and Opera Kitchen, located within the precinct, offer a range of dining options with picturesque views.

The Sydney Opera House is easily accessible, with various transportation options available, including trains, buses, and ferries. The Circular Quay train station and ferry terminal are conveniently located nearby, making it a central hub for exploring Sydney's attractions.

The Sydney Opera House stands as an architectural marvel, a cultural hub, and a symbol of national pride for Australia. Its distinct silhouette and contribution to the performing arts make it an essential destination for travelers seeking to immerse themselves in Australia's vibrant culture and history. Whether you explore its breathtaking exterior, take a guided tour, attend a performance, or simply soak in the surrounding beauty, the Sydney Opera House promises an unforgettable experience. As you plan your visit to Australia, ensure that the Sydney Opera House is a prominent feature on your itinerary, as it truly represents the epitome of art, architecture, and cultural expression.

Sydney Harbour Bridge

Australia is renowned for its stunning landscapes, rich history, and iconic landmarks. Among these, the Sydney Harbour Bridge stands tall as a symbol of architectural brilliance and a testament to human ingenuity. This magnificent steel arch bridge not only connects the bustling city of Sydney but also serves as a cherished tourist attraction and a significant part of Australia's cultural heritage. In this comprehensive travel guide, we will delve into the fascinating history, architectural marvels, and thrilling experiences that await visitors at the Sydney Harbour Bridge.

Historical Significance:

The Sydney Harbour Bridge holds a special place in Australia's history. Construction began in 1923 and concluded in 1932, during the height of the Great Depression. The bridge was a vital project that provided much-needed employment and became a symbol of hope for the Australian people. Known affectionately as the "Coathanger" due to its distinctive shape, the bridge was officially opened on March 19, 1932, by Premier Jack Lang.

Architectural Marvel:
The Sydney Harbour Bridge stands as a testament to human engineering prowess. Designed by British firm Dorman Long and Co. Ltd., in collaboration with Australian engineer John Bradfield, the bridge spans over 1,150 meters (3,772 feet) and reaches a height of 134 meters (440 feet) above the picturesque Sydney Harbour. The steel arch design not only ensures structural integrity but also creates a visually striking profile against the backdrop of the city skyline.

Bridge Climb Experience:
One of the most exhilarating ways to experience the Sydney Harbour Bridge is through the BridgeClimb. This unique adventure takes visitors on a guided tour to the summit of the bridge, providing breathtaking panoramic views of Sydney and its surroundings. Participants are equipped with safety gear and led by knowledgeable guides who share captivating stories about the bridge's

construction and its significance in Australian history. Whether it's witnessing a stunning sunrise or enjoying the vibrant city lights at night, the BridgeClimb offers an unforgettable experience for adrenaline enthusiasts and history buffs alike.

Pylon Lookout:

For those seeking an alternative to the BridgeClimb, the Pylon Lookout is a fantastic option. Located at the southeastern pylon of the bridge, the lookout offers a series of exhibits that showcase the bridge's construction, history, and its impact on the city. Visitors can climb the pylon to enjoy panoramic views of the Sydney Opera House, the harbor, and the city skyline. The Pylon Lookout is not only an educational experience but also a budget-friendly way to appreciate the grandeur of the Sydney Harbour Bridge.

Bridge Walks and Cycling:

In addition to the BridgeClimb and the Pylon Lookout, the Sydney Harbour Bridge provides pedestrian and cycling paths that allow visitors to traverse the bridge at their own pace. These paths offer an excellent opportunity to soak in the mesmerizing views and capture stunning photographs. Whether on foot or on a bicycle, the experience of crossing the bridge is truly unparalleled, offering a unique perspective of Sydney's harbor and iconic landmarks.

Vivid Sydney:

A highlight for visitors planning their trip to Sydney is the annual Vivid Sydney festival. Held during May and June, this vibrant festival transforms the city into a mesmerizing canvas of lights, music, and creativity. The Sydney Harbour Bridge becomes the centerpiece of this spectacular event, with its arches adorned in dazzling light displays that dance across the night sky. Witnessing the illuminated bridge during Vivid Sydney is a must-do experience for anyone visiting Australia's largest city.

Bridge Museum and Interpretive Center:

For those eager to delve deeper into the history and engineering behind the Sydney Harbour Bridge, a visit to the Bridge Museum and Interpretive Center is highly recommended. Located in the southern pylon, this interactive museum offers an immersive experience, allowing visitors to explore the bridge's construction process, view historical artifacts, and learn about the challenges faced during its creation. It's an educational opportunity to appreciate the bridge's significance and the remarkable feats achieved by the engineers and workers involved.

The Sydney Harbour Bridge stands as a remarkable testament to human engineering and serves as an enduring symbol of Australia's spirit and resilience. Whether admiring its grandeur from the waterfront, conquering its heights through the BridgeClimb, or exploring its history at the Pylon Lookout and Bridge Museum, the Sydney Harbour Bridge offers an unforgettable experience for travelers from all walks of life. As you plan your visit to Australia, make sure to include this iconic landmark in your itinerary to witness firsthand the magnificence of the Coathanger and create memories that will last a lifetime.

The Rocks

Situated at the southern end of the Sydney Harbour Bridge, The Rocks is one of the oldest and most historically significant neighborhoods in Sydney, Australia. This iconic precinct combines a rich colonial past with a vibrant contemporary atmosphere, making it a must-visit destination for travelers seeking a unique blend of history, culture, and entertainment. With its cobblestone streets, heritage buildings, lively markets, art galleries, and world-class dining options, The Rocks offers an enchanting experience that captures the essence of Sydney's past and present. In this travel guide, we will delve into the captivating story of The Rocks, exploring its attractions, events, and hidden gems.

Historical Background :

The history of The Rocks dates back to the arrival of the First Fleet in 1788, when European settlers established a penal colony in Sydney Cove. As the city's birthplace, The Rocks witnessed the struggles and triumphs of early colonial life, including convict settlements, outbreaks of disease, and social unrest. Over the years, the area grew and evolved, serving as a hub for maritime trade and a bustling working-class neighborhood.

However, in the 20th century, The Rocks faced the threat of demolition as urban development plans were put forward. The local community rallied together, forming the "Save Our Rocks" campaign, which successfully preserved the area's heritage buildings and paved the way for its revitalization. Today, The Rocks stands as a testament to the city's past and a testament to the importance of preserving historical sites.

Exploring The Rocks :

A stroll through the narrow laneways and cobblestone streets of The Rocks reveals a treasure trove of heritage buildings, boutique shops, and hidden gems. Start your exploration at the Rocks Discovery Museum, which provides a fascinating insight into the area's convict past and indigenous heritage.

One of the most iconic landmarks in The Rocks is the Sydney Observatory, where visitors can delve into the mysteries of the universe through interactive exhibits and stargazing sessions. For panoramic views of the harbor and city skyline, climb the Sydney Harbour Bridge Pylon Lookout, which offers a more affordable alternative to the BridgeClimb experience.

To experience the vibrant atmosphere of The Rocks, visit the weekend markets held at the historic Jack Mundey Place. Here, you can browse through a plethora of stalls selling unique arts and crafts, vintage clothing, and gourmet food. The Rocks also hosts numerous festivals and events throughout the year, including the Sydney Writers' Festival and the

Rocks Aroma Festival, a celebration of coffee and chocolate.

For art enthusiasts, The Rocks boasts a thriving art scene. Explore the numerous galleries, such as the Ken Done Gallery and the Artsite Galleries, which showcase contemporary and indigenous artworks. You can also participate in art workshops and engage with local artists to gain a deeper understanding of their creative processes.

Dining and Entertainment :

The Rocks offers an array of dining options to suit every palate, from quaint cafes to award-winning restaurants. Take a culinary journey through Australia's diverse flavors at The Rocks' renowned restaurants, such as Quay, serving modern Australian cuisine with a focus on local produce and innovative techniques. Alternatively, indulge in fresh seafood at the iconic Doyles on the Wharf, a family-owned institution that has been serving delicious seafood since 1885.

After satisfying your taste buds, enjoy a lively night out at one of the area's pubs or bars. The Rocks boasts historic establishments like The Lord Nelson Brewery Hotel, the oldest continually licensed hotel in Sydney, where you can sample their own handcrafted beers. For a more contemporary experience, head to The Argyle, a popular entertainment venue offering a mix of live music, DJ sets, and themed nights.

Accommodation and Transportation :

When it comes to accommodation, The Rocks offers a range of options to suit various budgets and preferences. From luxury hotels with stunning harbor views to cozy boutique bed and breakfasts tucked away in heritage buildings, there is something for everyone. Some notable establishments include the Park Hyatt Sydney, Pier One Sydney Harbour, and the Russell Hotel.

In terms of transportation, The Rocks is conveniently located within walking distance of Sydney's central business district, making it easily accessible on foot. For those who prefer public transport, Circular Quay train station and ferry terminal are just a stone's throw away, providing connections to other parts of the city and beyond.

The Rocks is a captivating neighborhood that effortlessly blends history, culture, and modern vibrancy. Its cobblestone streets, heritage buildings, and lively atmosphere make it a must-visit destination for travelers exploring Sydney. From delving into its convict past at the Rocks Discovery Museum to indulging in culinary delights at its world-class restaurants, there is something for everyone in this charming precinct.

The preservation of The Rocks showcases the importance of valuing and protecting our historical heritage, offering visitors a unique glimpse into Sydney's colonial history. Whether you're seeking a leisurely stroll through its laneways, an immersive art experience, or a vibrant night out, The Rocks will not disappoint.

As you explore The Rocks, remember to take the time to engage with the local community, appreciate the craftsmanship of its heritage buildings, and immerse yourself in the stories that have shaped this iconic precinct. Sydney's heart beats in The Rocks, where the past and present harmoniously converge, creating an unforgettable experience for all who visit.

Bondi Beach

Sydney, Australia, is known for its stunning beaches, and Bondi Beach is undoubtedly one of its most famous and iconic destinations. Situated just a few kilometers east of Sydney's central business district, Bondi Beach has been captivating locals and tourists alike for over a century. With its golden sands, sparkling blue waters, and vibrant beach culture, Bondi offers a unique and memorable experience for travelers seeking sun, surf, and relaxation. In this comprehensive Australia travel guide, we will delve into the history, attractions, activities, and practical information that will help you make the most of your visit to Bondi Beach.

History and Cultural Significance

Bondi Beach holds a significant place in Australian history and culture. The word "Bondi" originates from an Aboriginal word, "Boondi," meaning "water breaking over rocks." The beach has long been a gathering place for the local Indigenous Gadigal people, who have a deep connection to the land and the ocean.

In the late 19th century, Bondi Beach started to gain popularity as a seaside retreat. In 1882, the first public bathing pavilion was constructed, marking the beginning of organized swimming at Bondi. The beach's reputation as a fashionable destination grew in the early 20th century, attracting well-to-do residents who built extravagant homes overlooking the coastline.

Bondi Beach gained international recognition when it hosted the beach volleyball competition during the 2000 Sydney Olympic Games. Today, it continues to draw visitors from around the world who come to experience its vibrant atmosphere, coastal beauty, and thriving surf scene.

Beach and Surroundings

Stretching for approximately one kilometer, Bondi Beach boasts a crescent-shaped shoreline framed by picturesque cliffs and rocky headlands. The soft golden sand invites visitors to relax, sunbathe, and soak up the lively atmosphere. Lifeguards patrol the beach year-round, ensuring the safety of swimmers and surfers.

The coastal promenade, Campbell Parade, runs parallel to the beach and is lined with an array of cafes, restaurants, bars, and boutique shops. This bustling thoroughfare is a hub of activity, particularly during weekends and holidays when both locals and tourists flock to Bondi.

Bondi Icebergs Pool, an iconic ocean pool located at the southern end of the beach, is a must-visit attraction. Dating back to 1929, the pool offers stunning panoramic views of the beach and the Pacific Ocean. Visitors can take a refreshing dip in the saltwater pool or simply enjoy a meal at the adjacent Icebergs Dining

Room and Bar, which overlooks the pool and offers a fantastic dining experience.

Surfing is an integral part of Bondi's culture, and the beach is renowned for its consistent waves that cater to all skill levels. Whether you're a beginner wanting to take a surf lesson or an experienced surfer looking for a challenging break, there are numerous surf schools and board rental shops available to fulfill your needs.

Bondi also serves as a starting point for the breathtaking Bondi to Coogee Coastal Walk. This six-kilometer scenic trail winds along the coastline, passing through stunning beaches, parks, and cliffs. It offers panoramic views and opportunities to spot wildlife, making it a popular choice for nature enthusiasts and fitness enthusiasts alike.

Activities and Attractions

Beyond swimming and surfing, Bondi Beach offers a plethora of activities and attractions to keep visitors entertained. The Bondi Markets, held every Sunday, are a treasure trove of fashion, accessories, art, and organic produce. Exploring the markets is a great way to support local artisans and indulge in some retail therapy.

For art lovers, the Bondi Pavilion is a cultural hub hosting exhibitions, workshops, and live performances. It also houses the Bondi Pavilion Gallery, which showcases the works of local and international artists.

If you're interested in learning about Bondi's history and cultural significance, a visit to the Bondi Beach Historical Murals is a must. These vibrant murals depict significant moments and personalities from Bondi's past and present, providing an insight into the beach's rich heritage.

Bondi is also renowned for its vibrant dining scene. From casual beachside cafes to world-class restaurants, there is an abundance of options to satisfy every palate. Bondi's proximity to the ocean ensures a delightful array of fresh seafood choices, and the multicultural nature of Sydney is reflected in the diverse culinary offerings.

For those seeking relaxation and rejuvenation, Bondi offers several day spas and wellness centers. Indulge in a massage, practice yoga on the beach, or take part in a meditation class to find inner peace amidst the coastal beauty.

Practical Information

Getting to Bondi Beach is relatively easy, with various transportation options available. From

Sydney's city center, visitors can catch a bus or a train to Bondi Junction and then transfer to a connecting bus that takes them directly to the beach. Taxis and rideshare services are also readily available.

Accommodation options near Bondi Beach cater to all budgets and preferences. From luxurious beachfront hotels and boutique guesthouses to backpacker hostels and self-contained apartments, there is a wide range of choices to suit every traveler.

It is important to note that Bondi Beach can get crowded, especially during weekends and peak holiday periods. If you prefer a quieter experience, consider visiting during weekdays or in the shoulder seasons.

When visiting Bondi, it is essential to follow the beach safety guidelines provided by the lifeguards. Always swim between the flags, as they indicate the safest areas for swimming. It is also crucial to apply sunscreen regularly, wear a hat, and stay hydrated, as the Australian sun can be intense.

Bondi Beach is a quintessential Australian destination that offers an irresistible blend of natural beauty, vibrant culture, and exhilarating activities. Whether you're seeking a sun-soaked beach retreat, thrilling surf adventures, or a taste of Sydney's coastal lifestyle, Bondi Beach has it all. With its rich history, stunning surroundings, and an array of attractions and activities, a visit to Bondi Beach is an absolute must for any traveler exploring Sydney, Australia. So grab your sunscreen, embrace the laid-back vibes, and immerse yourself in the magic of Bondi Beach.

• *Activities and Entertainment*

Sydney, the vibrant capital of New South Wales, is a city renowned for its iconic landmarks, stunning beaches, and thriving cultural scene. With its diverse range of activities and entertainment options, Sydney offers something for everyone. Whether you're an outdoor enthusiast, a lover of the arts, or a foodie seeking culinary delights, this guide will provide you with a detailed overview of the best activities and entertainment options in Sydney.

Landmarks and Attractions:
Sydney is home to several world-famous landmarks that are must-visit destinations for any traveler. The Sydney Opera House, with its distinctive sail-like architecture, is an architectural masterpiece and a UNESCO

World Heritage site. Take a guided tour or catch a performance to experience the grandeur of this iconic venue. Adjacent to the Opera House is the Sydney Harbour Bridge, an engineering marvel that offers breathtaking views of the city skyline. Visitors can climb the bridge's arches for a thrilling adventure and unparalleled vistas.

For nature lovers, a visit to the Royal Botanic Garden is a must. Explore the lush gardens, enjoy a picnic by the water, or take a leisurely stroll while admiring the diverse flora and fauna. Bondi Beach, one of Sydney's most famous beaches, is perfect for sunbathing, surfing, and people-watching. Don't miss the opportunity to embark on the scenic Bondi to Coogee Coastal Walk, a picturesque six-kilometer trail that showcases stunning ocean views.

Cultural and Artistic Experiences:

Sydney boasts a vibrant arts and culture scene that offers a wide range of experiences. The Art Gallery of New South Wales houses an extensive collection of Australian and international artworks. From indigenous art to contemporary exhibitions, the gallery provides a rich cultural experience for art enthusiasts.

For a taste of history, visit The Rocks, Sydney's oldest neighborhood. Wander through its cobblestone streets, explore the historic buildings, and discover local artisans at the weekend markets. The Museum of Contemporary Art Australia, located in The Rocks, showcases cutting-edge contemporary artworks and hosts various exhibitions and events throughout the year.

Performing Arts and Entertainment:
Sydney's performing arts scene is thriving, with numerous theaters and venues offering world-class entertainment. The Capitol Theatre, a grand heritage-listed venue, hosts musicals, ballet performances, and concerts. The Sydney Lyric Theatre at The Star is another popular venue, known for its Broadway-style productions and blockbuster shows.

For a unique experience, head to the Sydney Opera House, which hosts a diverse range of performances, including opera, ballet, theater, and concerts. The annual Sydney Festival, held in January, showcases a fusion of local and international talent in a celebration of music, art, and performance.

Sporting Events:

Sydney is a city passionate about sports, and attending a live sporting event is a quintessential Australian experience. The Sydney Cricket Ground (SCG) is an iconic venue that hosts cricket matches during summer and Australian Rules Football in winter. The Olympic Park precinct, built for the 2000 Summer Olympics, is home to ANZ Stadium and Qudos Bank Arena, hosting major sporting events, concerts, and entertainment shows throughout the year.

Food and Dining:

Sydney is a culinary hotspot, offering an array of dining options to suit all tastes. The city is known for its multicultural cuisine, with a particular focus on fresh seafood. Indulge in a seafood feast at the Sydney Fish Market, the largest of its kind in the Southern Hemisphere.

For a multicultural food experience, head to Chinatown or the vibrant neighborhoods of Surry Hills and Newtown, where you'll find an eclectic mix of international flavors. Additionally, Sydney's vibrant café culture is not to be missed, with numerous trendy cafes serving up excellent coffee and brunch options.

Nightlife and Entertainment:

Sydney comes alive at night, offering a diverse range of nightlife and entertainment options. The Rocks and Darling Harbour are popular areas with a vibrant bar scene, live music venues, and clubs. King Street Wharf, located on the waterfront, is a hub of restaurants, bars, and nightclubs that offer stunning views of the harbor.

For those seeking a more relaxed evening, enjoy a sunset cocktail at one of the city's rooftop bars or take a nighttime cruise on Sydney Harbour to admire the city's sparkling skyline.

Sydney is a city that captivates visitors with its natural beauty, cultural richness, and vibrant entertainment options. From iconic landmarks to world-class performances, outdoor adventures to culinary delights, this guide has highlighted some of the best activities and entertainment experiences Sydney has to offer. Whether you're a first-time visitor or a returning traveler, Sydney promises a memorable journey filled with excitement and unforgettable moments.

•*Dining and Nightlife*

Sydney, the vibrant and cosmopolitan capital city of New South Wales, Australia, is renowned for its stunning harbor, iconic landmarks, and beautiful beaches. Beyond its natural beauty, Sydney offers a diverse and thriving dining and nightlife scene that caters to all tastes and preferences. From fine dining restaurants serving world-class cuisine to trendy bars and clubs, Sydney provides an unforgettable experience for locals and tourists alike. In this Australia travel guide, we will explore the rich tapestry of dining and nightlife options that Sydney has to offer.

Dining Experiences in Sydney:

Fine Dining: Sydney boasts a plethora of award-winning fine dining restaurants that showcase the city's culinary excellence. Quay, located at the Overseas Passenger Terminal in Circular Quay, offers breathtaking views of the Sydney Opera House while serving contemporary Australian cuisine. Tetsuya's, situated in a heritage-listed site in the CBD, is renowned for its Japanese-French fusion dishes and impeccable service. Sepia, in the heart of the city, presents a unique blend of flavors and textures in its modern

Australian cuisine.

Seafood: As a coastal city, Sydney is famous for its fresh seafood. The Sydney Fish Market, the largest of its kind in the Southern Hemisphere, is a must-visit destination for seafood lovers. Here, you can indulge in a wide variety of fish, prawns, oysters, and more. For a fine dining seafood experience, head to Cirrus Dining in Barangaroo, known for its innovative seafood-centric menu and stunning waterfront views.

Multicultural Cuisine: Sydney's multicultural population has contributed to a diverse culinary landscape. Explore the bustling streets of Chinatown for delicious Chinese delicacies, from dim sum to Peking duck. The vibrant suburb of Newtown offers a range of international cuisines, including Thai, Vietnamese, Indian, and Ethiopian. For a taste of the Mediterranean, visit Leichhardt, also known as "Little Italy," and savor authentic Italian dishes.

Cafés and Brunch Culture: Sydney's café culture is thriving, with numerous trendy cafés and brunch spots scattered throughout the city. Bondi Beach is a hotspot for breakfast and brunch options, with several beachside cafés offering healthy and innovative menus. The inner-city suburbs of Surry Hills and Paddington also house charming cafés known for their specialty coffee, freshly baked pastries, and delicious brunch fare.

Food Markets: Sydney's food markets are a hub of culinary delights. The Rocks Market, held every weekend, offers a range of gourmet food stalls, showcasing local produce and artisanal products. The Carriageworks Farmers Market in Eveleigh is another popular choice, featuring an array of organic and sustainable produce. These markets are ideal for sampling local flavors and mingling with the friendly Sydneysiders.

Nightlife in Sydney:

Bars and Pubs: Sydney's bar scene caters to all tastes, whether you're seeking a sophisticated cocktail lounge or a laid-back pub. The CBD and Surry Hills are home to many trendy bars, including Eau de Vie, a hidden speakeasy-style bar known for its creative cocktails. The Rocks precinct offers historic pubs where you can enjoy a pint of locally brewed craft beer while soaking up the city's rich history.

Rooftop Bars: Sydney's stunning skyline provides the perfect backdrop for rooftop bars.

The Ivy, located in the heart of the CBD, boasts several rooftop bars, including Pool Club and Ivy Penthouse, where you can sip cocktails while enjoying panoramic views of the city. Coogee Pavilion Rooftop, overlooking the famous Coogee Beach, offers a relaxed atmosphere and beachside vibes.

Live Music: Sydney has a thriving live music scene with venues catering to various genres. The Enmore Theatre in Newtown is a historic venue known for hosting local and international acts. Oxford Art Factory in Darlinghurst showcases emerging artists, while the iconic Sydney Opera House hosts a range of performances, from classical music to contemporary bands.

Casino: For those seeking a glamorous and entertaining night out, The Star Sydney is the city's premier casino complex. Located in Pyrmont, this venue offers a wide range of gaming options, fine dining restaurants, and lively bars. The Star also hosts live shows and events, adding to the excitement of the night.

Nightclubs: Sydney's nightlife wouldn't be complete without its vibrant nightclub scene. Kings Cross, Darlinghurst, and the CBD are the main areas where you can find some of the city's most popular nightclubs, including Home The Venue and Marquee Sydney. These venues feature world-class DJs, energetic dance floors, and state-of-the-art sound systems, providing an unforgettable clubbing experience.

Sydney's dining and nightlife scene is a testament to the city's diversity and vibrant culture. Whether you're a food enthusiast, a cocktail connoisseur, or a music lover, Sydney offers an extensive array of options to satisfy all tastes. From fine dining restaurants to casual eateries, rooftop bars to underground clubs, the city provides an unforgettable experience for travelers looking to immerse themselves in Sydney's culinary and nocturnal delights.

•*Shopping in Sydney*

Sydney, the vibrant capital city of New South Wales, Australia, is not only famous for its stunning landmarks and natural beauty but also for its diverse shopping scene. From luxury brands to local boutiques and bustling markets, Sydney offers a shopaholic's paradise. This Australia travel guide will take you on a virtual tour of the best shopping destinations in

Sydney, showcasing a variety of retail experiences that cater to every taste and budget.

Iconic Shopping Precincts:

a) Pitt Street Mall: Located in the heart of Sydney's central business district (CBD), Pitt Street Mall is a pedestrianized shopping strip that boasts flagship stores of international and Australian brands. From iconic department stores like David Jones and Myer to high-end labels such as Chanel and Louis Vuitton, this bustling mall is a shopaholic's dream come true.

b) Queen Victoria Building (QVB): Step into a world of elegance and grandeur at the QVB, a beautifully restored 19th-century building that houses a stunning array of boutiques, jewelry stores, and specialty shops. Admire the intricate architecture while browsing through designer labels like Alannah Hill, Carla Zampatti, and Oroton.

c) The Strand Arcade: Another historic shopping destination, The Strand Arcade, offers a unique shopping experience with its charming Victorian-era architecture. Explore its exquisite boutiques and discover Australian fashion designers, including Zimmermann and

Lover. The arcade is also known for its high-quality jewelry, accessories, and homeware stores.

Fashion and Lifestyle:

a) Oxford Street: Renowned for its fashion-forward boutiques and trendy stores, Oxford Street is the go-to destination for fashion enthusiasts. Discover a mix of local designers, independent labels, and vintage stores offering unique pieces that reflect Sydney's vibrant fashion scene.

b) Paddington Markets: Held every Saturday, Paddington Markets is a treasure trove of eclectic fashion, jewelry, art, and homeware stalls. Support local designers and artisans as you browse through the vibrant market stalls and soak up the lively atmosphere.

c) Westfield Sydney: For a comprehensive shopping experience, head to Westfield Sydney, a modern shopping center housing a wide range of international and Australian brands. From high street fashion to luxury labels, you'll find everything you need under one roof.

Unique Shopping Experiences:

a) The Rocks Markets: Immerse yourself in the historical charm of The Rocks, Sydney's oldest neighborhood, and explore its vibrant weekend markets. Discover unique handmade crafts, art, and souvenirs while enjoying live music and delicious street food.

b) Glebe Markets: Located in the bohemian suburb of Glebe, these markets offer a mix of vintage fashion, second-hand books, handmade jewelry, and organic produce. Enjoy the laid-back atmosphere and the chance to uncover hidden gems.

c) Paddy's Markets: Situated in Haymarket, Paddy's Markets is a bustling market where you can find a wide range of products, including clothing, accessories, fresh produce, and souvenirs. Bargain hunters will delight in the opportunity to haggle and find great deals.

Luxury Shopping:
a) Castlereagh Street: Known as Sydney's "Luxury Avenue," Castlereagh Street is lined with high-end fashion boutiques and flagship stores of prestigious brands such as Chanel, Gucci, and Dior. Indulge in a luxury shopping experience as you explore this upscale precinct.

b) The Intersection, Paddington: Nestled in the trendy suburb of Paddington, The Intersection showcases a curated collection of Australian designers, including Dion Lee, Christopher Esber, and Matin Studio. Experience the best of Australian fashion and immerse yourself in the local design scene.

Shopping in Sydney offers a diverse and exciting experience for visitors from around the world. Whether you're seeking luxury brands, local designer labels, or unique market finds, Sydney's shopping precincts have something for everyone. Soak up the vibrant atmosphere, indulge in retail therapy, and take home stylish mementos from your Australian adventure. Happy shopping!

•Day Trips from Sydney

Sydney, the vibrant capital of New South Wales, Australia, is not only renowned for its iconic landmarks like the Sydney Opera House and Sydney Harbour Bridge but also for its proximity to diverse natural landscapes and cultural attractions. With an extensive transportation network, it is easy to embark on exciting day trips from Sydney to explore the beauty and richness of the surrounding regions. This Australia travel guide provides a comprehensive overview of the top day trips from Sydney, highlighting the must-visit destinations within a day's reach.

Blue Mountains National Park:

Located just 50 kilometers west of Sydney, the Blue Mountains National Park offers breathtaking vistas, ancient rock formations, and lush eucalyptus forests. Visitors can marvel at the iconic Three Sisters rock formation in Katoomba, take scenic bushwalks along the numerous trails, or ride the steepest passenger railway in the world at Scenic World. The Blue Mountains also provide opportunities for adventure activities such as abseiling, canyoning, and rock climbing.

Hunter Valley Wine Region:

For wine enthusiasts, a day trip to the Hunter Valley is a must. Situated approximately two hours north of Sydney, this renowned wine region is home to over 150 wineries, picturesque vineyards, and charming cellar doors. Visitors can indulge in wine tastings, sample gourmet cuisine at award-winning restaurants, and take in the scenic beauty of the countryside. The Hunter Valley also offers hot air balloon rides, golf courses, and spa retreats for a truly relaxing and luxurious experience.

Royal National Park:

As the oldest national park in Australia, the Royal National Park is an idyllic escape located just south of Sydney. It offers a diverse range of activities, including coastal hikes, picturesque swimming spots, and stunning cliff-top lookouts. Visitors can explore the iconic Figure Eight Pools, embark on the Coastal Track for panoramic ocean views, or enjoy a picnic amidst the park's tranquil surroundings. Wildlife enthusiasts can spot native animals such as wallabies, echidnas, and bird species in their natural habitat.

Port Stephens:

Situated approximately two and a half hours north of Sydney, Port Stephens is a coastal paradise known for its pristine beaches, sand dunes, and abundant marine life. The region offers a plethora of activities, including dolphin and whale watching cruises, sandboarding on the Stockton Bight Sand Dunes, and snorkeling or diving in the marine sanctuaries. For adrenaline seekers, there are options for quad biking, parasailing, and jet skiing. Port

Stephens is also a haven for seafood lovers, with fresh oysters being a local specialty.

Jervis Bay:
Jervis Bay, located around 200 kilometers south of Sydney, boasts some of the whitest sands and clearest waters in the world. Visitors can relax on Hyams Beach, famous for its powdery sand, or take a leisurely coastal walk to admire the breathtaking coastal cliffs and rock formations. Jervis Bay is a haven for marine life, with opportunities for dolphin and seal cruises, snorkeling, and diving in the crystal-clear waters. The nearby Booderee National Park offers cultural experiences, bushwalks, and camping facilities for nature enthusiasts.

Canberra:
Although not technically a day trip, a visit to the nation's capital, Canberra, is highly recommended for those interested in Australian history and culture. Just a three-hour drive from Sydney, Canberra is home to numerous national museums, galleries, and landmarks, including the Australian War Memorial, National Gallery of Australia, and Parliament House. Visitors can explore the planned city's beautifully

landscaped parks, enjoy the vibrant food and wine scene, and immerse themselves in the country's political and cultural heritage.

Sydney's prime location offers an abundance of day trip opportunities that cater to a wide range of interests, from natural wonders to cultural experiences. Whether it's exploring the ancient Blue Mountains, savoring award-winning wines in the Hunter Valley, or basking in the coastal beauty of Jervis Bay, these day trips from Sydney provide unforgettable experiences for every traveler. So, plan your itinerary wisely and embark on these enriching adventures to discover the diverse beauty that surrounds Australia's iconic city.

CHAPTER FOUR

Melbourne

•*Overview of Melbourne*

Melbourne, the capital city of the state of Victoria, is a vibrant and cosmopolitan metropolis located in the southeastern part of Australia. Known for its unique blend of arts, culture, cuisine, and sports, Melbourne offers a captivating experience for travelers from around the world. From its iconic laneways adorned with street art to its world-class museums and picturesque parks, Melbourne has something to offer everyone. In this Australia travel guide, we will explore the various aspects that make Melbourne a must-visit destination.

1. *History and Culture:*

Melbourne has a rich history that dates back to its founding in 1835. Originally a small settlement, it quickly grew during the Victorian gold rush in the 1850s, becoming one of the wealthiest cities in the world at the time. Today, the city's history is evident in its magnificent architecture, such as the Victorian-era buildings that line its streets. The Aboriginal heritage of the region is also celebrated through various cultural events and landmarks, highlighting the city's diverse cultural fabric.

2. Architecture:

Melbourne's architecture is a captivating mix of old and new. The cityscape showcases a blend of heritage-listed buildings, such as Flinders Street Station and the Royal Exhibition Building, alongside modern marvels like Federation Square and the Eureka Tower. Exploring the city's architectural wonders is an adventure in itself, with each building telling a story of Melbourne's past and present.

3. Laneways and Street Art:

Melbourne is renowned for its vibrant laneways, which are narrow alleys that have been transformed into bustling hubs of creativity. Hosier Lane and AC/DC Lane are famous examples where you can immerse yourself in Melbourne's thriving street art scene. These laneways are adorned with colorful and ever-changing murals, making them perfect for Instagram-worthy photos and unique shopping experiences.

4. Food and Dining:

Melbourne has earned its reputation as Australia's food capital. With a diverse multicultural population, the city offers a remarkable culinary scene that caters to all tastes and budgets. From fine dining establishments to trendy cafes and bustling food markets, Melbourne is a haven for food lovers. Don't miss the opportunity to explore the hidden laneway cafes, sample international cuisines at Queen Victoria Market, or indulge in the famous coffee culture that Melbourne is known for.

5. Shopping:

Melbourne is a shopaholic's paradise, with a wide range of shopping options available. The city boasts several retail precincts, including Bourke Street Mall, Chapel Street, and Collins Street, where you can find high-end boutiques, designer labels, and flagship stores of renowned international brands. For a unique shopping experience, head to the Queen Victoria Market, which offers a vast selection of fresh produce, clothing, jewelry, and souvenirs.

6. Sports and Events:

Melbourne is often referred to as the sporting capital of Australia. The city hosts major international sporting events such as the Australian Open (tennis), Melbourne Cup (horse racing), and Australian Grand Prix (Formula 1). The iconic Melbourne Cricket Ground (MCG) is the largest stadium in the Southern Hemisphere and a must-visit for sports enthusiasts. Whether you want to watch a cricket match, Australian Rules football, or a tennis tournament, Melbourne has a thriving sports scene that will keep you entertained throughout the year.

7. Museums and Galleries:

Art and culture thrive in Melbourne, evident in its world-class museums and galleries. The National Gallery of Victoria (NGV) houses an extensive collection of Australian and international art, while the Australian Centre for the Moving Image (ACMI) showcases the history and evolution of film, television, and digital culture. The Melbourne Museum provides a fascinating insight into the natural and cultural history of the region, including the famous Bunjilaka Aboriginal

8. Parks and Gardens:

Melbourne is blessed with numerous parks and gardens, offering peaceful retreats within the bustling cityscape. The Royal Botanic Gardens, spanning over 94 acres, is a haven of lush greenery and stunning floral displays. Yarra Park, adjacent to the MCG, provides a tranquil space for picnics and leisurely strolls. For panoramic views of the city, head to the Royal Park or the Melbourne Star Observation Wheel.

9. Day Trips:

Beyond the city limits, Melbourne offers a plethora of day trip options. The Great Ocean Road, a scenic coastal drive, is a must-see, with highlights including the Twelve Apostles and the charming seaside towns of Lorne and Apollo Bay. The Yarra Valley, just an hour's drive from the city, is famous for its wineries and gourmet food experiences. Phillip Island is renowned for its penguin parade, where you can witness the adorable little penguins returning to their nests at sunset.

10. Festivals and Events:

Melbourne hosts a wide range of festivals and events throughout the year, showcasing its vibrant arts and cultural scene. The Melbourne

International Comedy Festival, the Melbourne International Film Festival, and the Moomba Festival are just a few of the events that attract visitors from near and far. These celebrations add to Melbourne's lively atmosphere and provide ample opportunities to immerse yourself in the local culture.

Melbourne is a city of endless possibilities. Its history, architecture, cultural diversity, and love for sports and arts combine to create a destination that truly captivates travelers. Whether you are a foodie, an art enthusiast, a sports fan, or simply seeking a memorable experience, Melbourne promises to leave you with lasting impressions and a desire to return for more.

•*Top Attractions*

Melbourne, the cultural capital of Australia, is a vibrant and cosmopolitan city that offers a wealth of attractions and experiences. With its rich history, diverse culture, and thriving arts scene, Melbourne is a must-visit destination for travelers. This comprehensive travel guide will take you on a journey through the top attractions in Melbourne, showcasing the city's unique blend of old-world charm and modern innovation.

1. Federation Square:

Located in the heart of Melbourne, Federation Square is a bustling cultural precinct that showcases the city's architectural prowess. This modern public space is home to numerous galleries, restaurants, and cultural events. The iconic Federation Square is an excellent starting point for exploring Melbourne's attractions, with its striking design and vibrant atmosphere.

2. Flinders Street Station:

A Melbourne landmark, Flinders Street Station is a stunning example of Victorian architecture. Built in 1854, it is the oldest train station in Australia and serves as a transportation hub for the city. The station's iconic yellow facade and grand clock tower make it a popular meeting point for locals and tourists alike.

3. Queen Victoria Market:

For a true taste of Melbourne, a visit to Queen Victoria Market is a must. This bustling open-air market has been operating since 1878 and offers a vast array of fresh produce, gourmet delights, clothing, and souvenirs.

Explore the vibrant stalls, indulge in delicious street food, and soak up the lively atmosphere of this iconic market.

4. Melbourne Museum:

Immerse yourself in Melbourne's rich history and culture at the Melbourne Museum. Located in Carlton Gardens, this world-class museum houses an extensive collection of artifacts, interactive exhibits, and displays showcasing the city's past, present, and future. Don't miss the famous Melbourne Story exhibition, which takes visitors on a journey through the city's development.

5. Royal Botanic Gardens:

Escape the hustle and bustle of the city at the serene Royal Botanic Gardens. Spanning over 38 hectares, these beautifully landscaped gardens offer a peaceful retreat with stunning views of the city skyline. Take a leisurely stroll, have a picnic, or join a guided tour to discover the diverse flora and fauna of this botanical paradise.

6. National Gallery of Victoria:

Art enthusiasts will be captivated by the National Gallery of Victoria (NGV), Australia's oldest and largest public art museum. The NGV features an extensive collection of international and Australian art, including works by renowned artists such as Picasso, Monet, and Indigenous Australian artists. With its diverse range of exhibitions and immersive installations, the NGV is a haven for art lovers.

7. Eureka Skydeck:

For panoramic views of Melbourne, head to the Eureka Skydeck, located on the 88th floor of the Eureka Tower. As the highest public vantage point in the Southern Hemisphere, the Skydeck offers breathtaking 360-degree views of the city. Dare to step onto "The Edge," a glass cube that extends from the building, providing a thrilling experience suspended above the city.

8. St. Kilda Beach:

Escape to the sandy shores of St. Kilda Beach, one of Melbourne's most popular coastal destinations. This vibrant beachside suburb offers a range of activities, from swimming and sunbathing to cycling along the promenade. Explore the famous Luna Park amusement park, indulge in delicious seafood, or simply relax and enjoy the stunning views of Port Phillip Bay.

9. Great Ocean Road:

While not directly in Melbourne, the Great Ocean Road is a breathtaking coastal drive that starts just outside the city. Stretching over 240 kilometers, this scenic road winds along the coast, offering stunning vistas of rugged cliffs, pristine beaches, and the iconic Twelve Apostles rock formations

10. Sports Precinct:

Melbourne is renowned for its passion for sports, and a visit to the sports precinct is a must for sports enthusiasts. Explore the hallowed grounds of the Melbourne Cricket Ground (MCG), which hosts cricket matches and Australian Rules Football games. Adjacent to the MCG, you'll find the National Sports Museum, where you can delve into the history of Australian sports through interactive exhibits and memorabilia.

Melbourne, with its diverse attractions and vibrant atmosphere, is a city that captures the essence of Australia's culture and spirit. From its architectural marvels and cultural institutions to its beautiful gardens and stunning coastal drives, Melbourne offers a wealth of experiences for every traveler.

Immerse yourself in the city's history, indulge in its culinary delights, and embrace the vibrant energy that permeates the streets of this captivating metropolis. Plan your visit to Melbourne and unlock the secrets of this thriving Australian city.

Federation Square

Federation Square, located in the heart of Melbourne, Australia, is a remarkable urban precinct that has become an iconic symbol of the city. Built to commemorate the centenary of Australia's federation in 2001, this architectural masterpiece has quickly established itself as a cultural hub, hosting a diverse range of events, exhibitions, and activities. With its striking design, rich cultural significance, and dynamic atmosphere, Federation Square has become a must-visit destination for tourists and locals alike. This travel guide aims to delve into the many facets of Federation Square, exploring its history, design, attractions, and the unique experiences it offers to visitors.

1. Historical Significance:

Federation Square holds immense historical significance for Australia. It was designed to celebrate the federation of the nation, which occurred on January 1, 1901. The square stands on the site where the first public reading of the Australian Constitution took place in 1900. As a result, it serves as a symbolic representation of the unity and diversity of the Australian people. Visitors can learn more about this history through informative displays and exhibitions at the onsite Australian Centre for the Moving Image (ACMI) and the Koorie Heritage Trust.

2. Architectural Marvel:

One cannot discuss Federation Square without marveling at its unique architectural design. Designed by renowned architects Lab Architecture Studio and Bates Smart, the precinct's unconventional layout features a juxtaposition of modern and abstract structures, using a combination of steel, glass, and sandstone. The unconventional design has won numerous architectural awards and draws visitors with its distinctive look. The square's centerpiece, the Ian Potter Centre: NGV Australia, showcases Australian art, while the nearby Australian Centre for Contemporary Art

(ACCA) features cutting-edge contemporary exhibitions.

3. Cultural Offerings:
Federation Square is a cultural mecca that hosts a wide range of events, performances, and exhibitions throughout the year. The ACMI is a popular attraction, dedicated to showcasing the rich history and future of Australian film, television, and digital culture. Visitors can explore interactive exhibits, attend screenings, and participate in workshops. The NGV Australia, housed within Federation Square, displays an extensive collection of Australian art, spanning from colonial times to the present day. The ACCA presents contemporary art exhibitions, challenging visitors with innovative and thought-provoking works.

4. Entertainment and Festivals:
The square is a hive of activity, offering a plethora of entertainment options. From live music performances and theatrical productions to outdoor screenings and public art displays, there is always something happening at Federation Square. The square's open-air amphitheater serves as a vibrant venue for concerts and cultural events. Additionally, Federation Square hosts several annual

festivals, including the vibrant cultural celebration of the Melbourne Festival and the popular White Night Melbourne, where the city comes alive with all-night art installations and performances.

5. Dining and Shopping:

Federation Square is home to a diverse range of dining establishments and retail outlets, catering to all tastes and preferences. Visitors can indulge in a variety of culinary experiences, ranging from casual cafes and food trucks to upscale restaurants offering world-class cuisine. The square also features a vibrant market, known as The Atrium, which showcases local artisans, crafts, and fresh produce. Whether it's grabbing a quick bite, enjoying a leisurely meal, or browsing unique boutique stores, Federation Square offers a delightful shopping and dining experience.

6. Connectivity and Accessibility:

Federation Square's central location makes it easily accessible to visitors. It is situated in close proximity to Melbourne's major transportation hubs, including Flinders Street Station and the tram network. The square serves as a convenient starting point for exploring the city's other attractions, such as the nearby Yarra River, the iconic Flinders Street Station, and the

bustling shopping precinct of Bourke Street Mall. Guided walking tours are available for those who wish to explore Federation Square's surroundings and delve deeper into Melbourne's history and culture.

Federation Square stands as a testament to Melbourne's vibrant arts and cultural scene. With its striking architecture, rich history, diverse cultural offerings, and lively atmosphere, it has become an essential destination for travelers seeking an authentic Australian experience. From exploring art galleries and attending live performances to indulging in culinary delights and soaking up the city's festive spirit, Federation Square offers a multitude of experiences to suit every taste. As you plan your trip to Melbourne, be sure to include Federation Square on your itinerary and immerse yourself in the energy and creativity that this captivating precinct has to offer.

Queen Victoria Market

Melbourne, the cultural capital of Australia, is known for its diverse culinary scene and vibrant markets. Among the numerous markets scattered throughout the city, the Queen Victoria Market stands as a crown jewel. Established in the late 19th century, this iconic landmark has become a must-visit destination for both locals and tourists alike. Spanning across seven hectares, the market is a bustling hub of fresh produce, delectable food stalls, unique merchandise, and a vibrant atmosphere. In this Australia travel guide, we will delve into the fascinating history, the diverse offerings, and the lively ambiance of the Queen Victoria Market.

A Historical Treasure:

The Queen Victoria Market holds a rich history that dates back to 1878 when it first opened its doors. Initially known as the Melbourne Cemetery, the site was repurposed to accommodate the growing demand for fresh produce and trade. Today, the market stands as a testament to Melbourne's past while embracing its thriving present. Despite undergoing various transformations over the years, it has retained its unique charm and character, making it one of Melbourne's most beloved landmarks.

Exploring the Market:

Covering a vast area, the Queen Victoria Market can be divided into several distinct sections, each offering a different experience.

1. The Food Market:
The heart and soul of the market lie within its food section. Here, visitors can find a plethora of fresh produce, meats, seafood, and specialty ingredients. The market prides itself on offering a wide array of seasonal fruits and vegetables, sourced both locally and internationally. It's a paradise for food enthusiasts, where one can sample exotic flavors, purchase quality ingredients, and engage with friendly vendors who are always happy to share their culinary expertise.

2. The Deli Hall:
For those with a penchant for gourmet delights, the Deli Hall is a treasure trove of cheeses, cured meats, olives, and other delicacies. The aroma of freshly baked bread wafts through the air as visitors peruse the various stalls, sampling their way through the assortment of

flavors. It's an ideal spot to pick up artisanal products or create a picnic basket for a delightful lunch in one of Melbourne's picturesque parks.

3. The Meat and Fish Hall:
Step into the Meat and Fish Hall, and you'll be greeted by a symphony of sights and smells. From succulent cuts of beef and lamb to the freshest seafood, this section caters to the needs of both home cooks and professional chefs. The market's skilled butchers and fishmongers offer expert advice and gladly assist in selecting the perfect cut or catch of the day.

4. The Victoria Street Shops:
As you wander through the Victoria Street Shops, you'll discover a treasure trove of clothing, accessories, souvenirs, and homeware. From locally designed fashion pieces to unique handcrafted items, this section showcases the creative talents of Melbourne's artisans. It's an ideal place to find a special memento or gift that encapsulates the essence of your visit to the city.

5. The Night Market:

During the summer months, the Queen Victoria Market comes alive with its vibrant Night Market. Every Wednesday evening, locals and tourists gather to experience the market's lively atmosphere after dark. Featuring live entertainment, street food stalls, and an eclectic mix of arts and crafts, the Night Market is a must-visit for those seeking an unforgettable Melbourne experience.

Cultural Significance:

The Queen Victoria Market holds immense cultural significance for the people of Melbourne. It has become a melting pot of diverse communities, reflecting the city's multicultural identity. Over the years, various cultural festivals and events have been held within the market, celebrating Melbourne's vibrant tapestry of cultures. From Chinese New Year celebrations to Diw

ali festivals, the market embraces and honors the traditions and customs of its diverse visitors.

Beyond the market's cultural events, it serves as a meeting place for locals to connect, socialize, and support local businesses. The community spirit is palpable, and a visit to the market provides a genuine sense of belonging and camaraderie.

Tips for Visitors:

1. Timing: The Queen Victoria Market is open five days a week, from Tuesday to Sunday. For the best experience, consider visiting on a weekday morning when it's less crowded, allowing you to explore at a leisurely pace.

2. Sample the Cuisine: Don't miss the opportunity to savor the diverse cuisine available at the market. From freshly shucked oysters to sizzling Asian stir-fries, there's something to satisfy every palate.

3. Engage with the Vendors: Strike up a conversation with the friendly vendors who are passionate about their products. They are a wealth of knowledge and can provide valuable insights into Melbourne's culinary scene.

4. Embrace the Night Market: If you happen to be in Melbourne during the summer, make sure to visit the Night Market for a vibrant evening filled with food, entertainment, and a lively atmosphere.

The Queen Victoria Market stands as an iconic landmark in Melbourne, capturing the essence of the city's vibrant culture and culinary heritage. With its rich history, diverse offerings, and lively atmosphere, it has become a must-visit destination for travelers seeking an authentic Melbourne experience. From the bustling food market to the charming Victoria Street Shops, the market offers a plethora of delights for visitors to explore. Immerse yourself in the vibrant atmosphere, indulge in delicious flavors, and discover the treasures that make the Queen Victoria Market an unforgettable destination in Australia's cultural capital.

Royal Botanic Gardens

Welcome to the enchanting realm of the Royal Botanic Gardens, a verdant oasis nestled in the heart of Melbourne, Australia. With a rich history dating back to 1846, these world-renowned gardens offer visitors an exquisite blend of botanical diversity, stunning landscapes, and cultural heritage. Spread across 94 acres, the Royal Botanic Gardens serve as a tranquil haven, inviting locals and tourists alike to immerse themselves in the beauty of nature. This Australia travel guide will take you on a captivating journey through the mesmerizing Royal Botanic Gardens, providing insights into its history, notable features, and must-visit attractions.

I. Historical Overview

The Royal Botanic Gardens in Melbourne have a captivating history that traces back to their establishment in 1846. Originally conceived as an experimental garden to acclimatize and cultivate useful plants, the gardens gradually evolved into a cherished cultural and recreational hub. Under the guidance of renowned botanist Ferdinand von Mueller, the gardens flourished, expanding their collection of plants and earning international acclaim.

II. Botanical Treasures

The Royal Botanic Gardens boast an extraordinary diversity of flora, comprising over 8,500 plant species from around the globe. Divided into various precincts, each with its distinct character, the gardens offer an immersive experience for plant enthusiasts, nature lovers, and casual visitors alike. Here are a few notable precincts within the gardens:

1. Australian Rainforest Walk:

This lush section showcases an array of indigenous plant species, including ancient ferns, towering eucalyptus trees, and vibrant flowering plants. Take a leisurely stroll along the well-marked paths, and marvel at the serene beauty of this captivating rainforest.

2. The Ian Potter Foundation Children's Garden:

Designed to ignite children's curiosity and love for nature, this interactive garden provides a fun-filled educational experience. With features like a bamboo forest, a misting rock, and a plant tunnel, children can engage in hands-on exploration and discover the wonders of the natural world.

3. Ornamental Lake:

Offering a picturesque setting, the Ornamental Lake is the centerpiece of the gardens. Visitors can enjoy leisurely boat rides, observe waterbirds in their natural habitat, or simply relax on the surrounding lawns while admiring the serene beauty of the lake.

4. Herb Garden:

Immerse yourself in the fragrant world of herbs as you wander through the Herb Garden. Discover a vast array of culinary, medicinal, and aromatic plants, and learn about their diverse uses and benefits.

III. Architectural Marvels

The Royal Botanic Gardens not only captivate with their natural beauty but also boast several architectural gems that enhance the overall charm of the landscape. These structures seamlessly blend with the surrounding flora and include:

1. The Terrace:

This elegant structure, adorned with intricate ironwork and a stunning façade, is a testament to Victorian-era architecture. Offering panoramic views of the gardens, it serves as an ideal spot for relaxation and contemplation.

2. Guilfoyle's Volcano:

An innovative water conservation project turned landmark, Guilfoyle's Volcano is an impressive display of Victorian-era garden design. This intriguing structure houses a collection of water-efficient plants, showcasing sustainable gardening practices.

IV. Cultural and Educational Significance

The Royal Botanic Gardens Melbourne play a pivotal role in preserving cultural heritage and promoting education about plants and the environment. The gardens offer a range of educational programs, guided tours, and exhibitions to engage visitors of all ages. Some notable attractions include:

1. Aboriginal Heritage Walk:
   Join an Indigenous

guide on a journey through the gardens, exploring the rich cultural heritage of the local Koolin nation. Learn about traditional uses of plants, ancient stories, and the deep connection between Aboriginal people and the land.

2. National Herbarium of Victoria:
   Situated within the gardens, the National Herbarium of Victoria houses a vast collection of dried plant specimens and serves as a valuable resource for scientific research and botanical studies.

3. Garden Explorer:

Embark on a guided tour aboard the Garden Explorer, an eco-friendly electric vehicle. This informative tour provides insights into the gardens' history, highlights key features, and unveils fascinating botanical facts.

V. Events and Activities

Throughout the year, the Royal Botanic Gardens host a variety of events and activities that cater to different interests. From music concerts to horticultural workshops, there is always something for everyone to enjoy. Some noteworthy events include:

1. Moonlight Cinema:

Experience the magic of outdoor cinema against the backdrop of the gardens. Snuggle up under the stars with loved ones and enjoy a selection of classic and contemporary films.

2. Botanic Nights:

An enchanting after-dark experience, Botanic Nights combines live music, art installations, and captivating lighting displays. Wander through the illuminated gardens and immerse yourself in the atmospheric ambiance.

The Royal Botanic Gardens Melbourne exemplify the perfect union between nature, history, and culture. Whether you are seeking a peaceful retreat, educational exploration, or a visual feast for the senses, these gardens offer an unforgettable experience. So, embark on a journey of discovery and immerse yourself in the splendor of the Royal Botanic Gardens, where the beauty of nature and the wonders of human creativity intertwine in perfect harmony.

St. Kilda Beach

Welcome to St. Kilda Beach, a picturesque seaside destination located in the vibrant city of Melbourne, Australia. With its pristine golden sands, sparkling blue waters, and an array of activities, St. Kilda Beach is a must-visit attraction for travelers from around the world. This comprehensive travel guide will take you on a journey through the history, natural beauty, exciting attractions, and vibrant atmosphere of St. Kilda Beach, ensuring that you make the most of your visit to this iconic Australian destination.

I. History and Location

Situated just 6 kilometers south-east of Melbourne's city center, St. Kilda Beach holds a significant place in Australia's history and cultural heritage. Named after the ship "Lady of St. Kilda" that anchored in the area in 1841, this beach has evolved from a humble fishing village into a thriving seaside suburb.

II. Natural Beauty and Climate

St. Kilda Beach boasts breathtaking natural beauty, making it a favorite spot for locals and tourists alike. The beach stretches over 700 meters and is adorned with soft, golden sands, perfect for sunbathing and leisurely strolls. The crystal-clear waters of Port Phillip Bay provide an ideal setting for swimming, sailing, and other water activities.

The beach is bordered by the iconic St. Kilda Pier, which offers panoramic views of the Melbourne skyline and is a popular spot for fishing enthusiasts. Nearby, you'll find the St. Kilda Botanical Gardens, a peaceful oasis filled with lush greenery, vibrant flowers, and tranquil walking paths.

Melbourne's temperate climate ensures that St. Kilda Beach is enjoyable throughout the year.

Summers (December to February) are warm, with temperatures ranging from 20 to 30 degrees Celsius (68 to 86 degrees Fahrenheit). Autumn (March to May) brings milder temperatures, while winters (June to August) are cool but rarely drop below 10 degrees Celsius (50 degrees Fahrenheit). Spring (September to November) is a delightful season, with blooming flowers and pleasant temperatures.

III. Attractions and Activities
a) Luna Park: One of St. Kilda's most iconic landmarks, Luna Park is an amusement park that has been delighting visitors since 1912. Its famous entrance, featuring a large clown face, is instantly recognizable. The park offers a range of thrilling rides, including roller coasters, Ferris wheels, and arcade games, making it an ideal destination for families and thrill-seekers alike.

b) St. Kilda Esplanade Market: Held every Sunday along the esplanade, this vibrant market is a treasure trove of local arts, crafts, clothing, and delicious street food. Browse through stalls filled with unique handmade jewelry, artworks, vintage clothing, and souvenirs, and savor the flavors of various cuisines from around the world.

c) St. Kilda Sea Baths: Located adjacent to the beach, the St. Kilda Sea Baths offer a fantastic blend of relaxation and recreation. The complex features heated saltwater pools, a hydrotherapy spa, steam rooms, and a gymnasium, allowing visitors to unwind and rejuvenate while enjoying panoramic views of the bay.

d) Penguin Colony: Head to the breakwater near St. Kilda Pier at dusk to witness a delightful spectacle—the arrival of the St. Kilda penguins. These adorable little creatures return from their day at sea to nest in the rocks, providing an enchanting experience for onlookers. Remember to observe from a respectful distance, as the penguins' well-being is of utmost importance.

e) Acland Street: Just a short walk from

the beach, Acland Street is a bustling thoroughfare known for its vibrant café culture, eclectic shops, and mouthwatering bakeries. Indulge in delectable cakes, pastries, and sweets at one of the iconic cake shops, and explore the boutiques, galleries, and bookstores that line the street.

f) Sports and Recreation: St. Kilda Beach offers ample opportunities for outdoor activities. Join a game of beach volleyball, take a leisurely bike ride along the foreshore, or try your hand at windsurfing or kiteboarding. The beachside promenade is perfect for jogging or rollerblading, while the grassy areas nearby are ideal for picnics and barbecues.

g) St. Kilda Festival: If you happen to visit in February, don't miss the St. Kilda Festival, Australia's largest free music festival. The festival features live performances by local and international artists, vibrant street parades, food stalls, and a lively carnival atmosphere that showcases the best of Melbourne's cultural scene.

IV. Dining and Nightlife
St. Kilda Beach is renowned for its diverse culinary scene, offering a wide range of dining options to suit every palate and budget. From casual beachside cafés to upscale seafood restaurants, you'll find a myriad of choices along the esplanade and surrounding streets.

For seafood lovers, Stokehouse offers a refined dining experience with panoramic bay views, while Claypots Seafood Bar is a local favorite for its fresh, flavorsome seafood served in a lively atmosphere. Vegans and vegetarians will be delighted by the plant-based delights at Sister of Soul, an award-winning restaurant renowned for its inventive and delicious dishes.

St. Kilda's nightlife scene is equally vibrant, with numerous bars, pubs, and clubs catering to different tastes. Enjoy live music at the iconic Prince Bandroom, dance the night away at the famous St. Kilda Beach Hotel, or savor craft beers at one of the area's trendy microbreweries. The options are endless, ensuring that visitors can find the perfect spot to unwind and enjoy Melbourne's renowned nightlife.

V. Accommodation and Transportation

St. Kilda offers a range of accommodation options to suit various budgets and preferences. From luxury hotels with stunning bay views to cozy boutique guesthouses and backpacker hostels, you'll find something to meet your needs. Some popular choices include the Novotel Melbourne St Kilda, Tolarno Hotel, and Habitat HQ Hostel.

Getting to St. Kilda Beach is convenient, thanks to Melbourne's extensive public transportation network. Trams provide easy access to the area, with several routes serving St. Kilda from the city center and other nearby suburbs. Additionally, buses and trains are available for further exploration of Melbourne and its surrounding regions.

St. Kilda Beach in Melbourne, Australia, encapsulates the essence of an idyllic coastal destination, offering a blend of natural beauty, exciting attractions, and a lively atmosphere. Whether you're seeking relaxation, adventure, or cultural experiences, St. Kilda Beach has something for everyone. From the nostalgic charm of Luna Park to the vibrant markets, picturesque penguins, and lively dining scene, this iconic beach is sure to leave an indelible impression on your Australian travel memories. So, pack your sunscreen, embrace the coastal vibes, and get ready to immerse yourself in the magic of St. Kilda Beach.

• *Activities and Entertainment*

Melbourne, the vibrant capital of the Australian state of Victoria, is known for its lively arts scene, multicultural atmosphere, and an array of activities and entertainment options. Whether you're a nature enthusiast, a sports fan, an art lover, or a foodie, Melbourne has something to offer for everyone. In this comprehensive travel guide, we will delve into the diverse range of activities and entertainment available in Melbourne, ensuring that your visit to this beautiful city is an unforgettable experience.

1. Cultural Delights:

Melbourne boasts a rich cultural heritage that can be explored through various activities and entertainment options:

a) Art Galleries and Museums:
Immerse yourself in Melbourne's thriving art scene by visiting renowned galleries like the National Gallery of Victoria (NGV), showcasing a vast collection of international and Australian artworks. The Ian Potter Centre: NGV Australia is a must-visit for those interested in indigenous art. Additionally, explore the Australian Centre for the Moving Image (ACMI) for a unique experience blending art, film, and digital culture.

b) Theatre and Performing Arts:

Melbourne is widely regarded as Australia's cultural hub, with a vibrant theatre and performing arts scene. Enjoy world-class productions at iconic venues like the Regent Theatre, Princess Theatre, and Arts Centre Melbourne. Don't miss the opportunity to witness the innovative performances at the Melbourne Theatre Company and the Victorian Opera.

c) Cultural Festivals:
Throughout the year, Melbourne hosts a range of festivals celebrating various cultures, including the Melbourne International Arts Festival, Moomba Festival, and the Chinese New Year celebrations in Chinatown. These events offer an immersive experience into the diverse cultural fabric of the city.

2. Sports and Outdoor Activities:
Melbourne is a haven for sports enthusiasts, offering a multitude of sports and outdoor activities:

a) Australian Rules Football:
Experience the electric atmosphere of Australian Rules Football by attending a match at the iconic Melbourne Cricket Ground (MCG). The Australian Football League (AFL)

season runs from March to September, with matches held throughout the city.

b) Cricket:
The MCG is also home to international cricket matches, including the renowned Boxing Day Test. Catch a game during the cricket season (October to March) and witness the excitement of this quintessential Australian sport.

c) Tennis:
Melbourne Park, home to the Australian Open, is a must-visit for tennis fans. The Grand Slam tournament takes place annually in January, attracting top-ranked players from around the world.

d) Outdoor Recreation:
Escape the urban buzz and explore Melbourne's natural beauty. Take a stroll through the Royal Botanic Gardens, go cycling along the Yarra River, or enjoy a picnic at the picturesque St Kilda Beach. For adventure seekers, the Dandenong Ranges and the Great Ocean Road offer breathtaking landscapes and hiking opportunities.

3. Food and Dining:

Melbourne has gained international recognition as a food lover's paradise, boasting a diverse culinary scene:

a) Laneway Dining:
Discover Melbourne's hidden culinary gems in the city's laneways and alleys. Explore Degraves Street, Centre Place, and Hardware Lane, where you'll find cozy cafes, trendy bars, and international cuisine.

b) Food Markets:
Visit the Queen Victoria Market, an iconic landmark offering a vast array of fresh produce, gourmet delights, and local delicacies. The South Melbourne Market is another popular destination for food enthusiasts, showcasing a blend of local and international flavors.

c) Brunch Culture:
Melbourne is renowned for its brunch culture. Enjoy a leisurely morning at one of the city's trendy brunch spots, savoring delectable dishes accompanied by exceptional coffee.

4. Shopping and Entertainment:
Melbourne offers a diverse range of shopping and entertainment options,

catering to all tastes:

a) Shopping Precincts:
Discover Melbourne's fashion scene by exploring shopping precincts like Bourke Street Mall, Chapel Street, and Collins Street. These areas are lined with designer boutiques, department stores, and unique independent retailers.

b) Entertainment Complexes:
Crown Melbourne, located on the banks of the Yarra River, is a world-class entertainment complex featuring a casino, luxury hotels, upscale restaurants, and live entertainment venues. It is a one-stop destination for those seeking excitement and glamour.

c) Nightlife:
Melbourne's nightlife is vibrant and diverse, with numerous bars, pubs, and clubs scattered throughout the city. Whether you're into rooftop bars with panoramic views, hidden speakeasies, or live music venues, Melbourne's nightlife scene has something for everyone.

Melbourne, Australia's cultural capital, offers an array of activities and entertainment options that cater to all interests. From immersing yourself in the city's vibrant arts scene to exploring the great outdoors, indulging in diverse culinary delights, or enjoying thrilling sports events, Melbourne ensures a memorable experience for every traveler. So, plan your visit to Melbourne and get ready to discover the dynamic city that effortlessly combines culture, sports, entertainment, and natural beauty.

• *Dining and Nightlife*

Melbourne, the cultural capital of Australia, is renowned for its thriving dining and nightlife scene. This cosmopolitan city boasts a diverse culinary landscape that caters to all tastes and budgets. From trendy rooftop bars and hidden laneway eateries to world-class fine dining establishments, Melbourne offers an unforgettable gastronomic experience. In this travel guide, we will explore the city's vibrant dining and nightlife scene, highlighting its iconic restaurants, popular food precincts, and exciting entertainment options.

1. *Iconic Dining Experiences*
Melbourne is home to a plethora of iconic dining experiences that have earned

international acclaim. For those seeking an unforgettable fine dining experience, the city boasts an impressive array of Michelin-starred restaurants. Vue de Monde, located atop the Rialto Tower, offers breathtaking views of the city skyline and a contemporary Australian menu that showcases the finest local ingredients.

For a taste of culinary innovation, visit Attica in Ripponlea. Renowned chef Ben Shewry crafts a unique menu inspired by Australian landscapes, presenting dishes that are both visually stunning and deliciously inventive. Lûmé in South Melbourne is another top-notch dining destination, renowned for its avant-garde approach to gastronomy.

2. Laneways and Hidden Gems

Melbourne's laneways are a treasure trove of hidden gems waiting to be discovered by food enthusiasts. Explore the famous Centre Place, Degraves Street, and Hardware Lane, where charming cafes and bistros spill out onto the cobblestoned lanes. These laneways offer an array of international cuisines, including Italian, Japanese, Greek, and Middle Eastern, catering to diverse palates.

Don't miss Queen Victoria Market, a vibrant hub where you can sample local produce and indulge in street food delights. Food trucks and stalls offer a wide range of culinary treats, from gourmet burgers to fresh seafood. The market also hosts night markets during the summer months, where visitors can enjoy live music, entertainment, and a buzzing atmosphere.

3. Vibrant Food Precincts

Melbourne is renowned for its diverse and dynamic food precincts that cater to different tastes and budgets. Explore the multicultural flavors of Victoria Street in Richmond, often referred to as "Little Saigon." This bustling strip is lined with Vietnamese restaurants and grocery stores, offering authentic dishes such as pho and banh mi.

For a taste of Italy, head to Lygon Street in Carlton, known as Melbourne's "Little Italy." This vibrant precinct is home to traditional Italian trattorias, gelaterias, and espresso bars. Indulge in wood-fired pizzas, hearty pasta dishes, and decadent desserts while immersing yourself in the rich Italian culture.

Fitzroy and Collingwood are trendy suburbs that have gained popularity for their thriving food scenes. Smith Street in Collingwood is dotted with hip cafes, trendy bars, and innovative eateries, making it a must-visit for foodies seeking the latest culinary trends.

4. Rooftop Bars and Cocktail Culture
Melbourne is famous for its rooftop bars, offering breathtaking views of the city skyline and a vibrant atmosphere. The Rooftop at QT is a popular choice, with its stylish decor, refreshing cocktails, and panoramic views of the city. Lui Bar, located on the 55th floor of the Rialto Tower, offers a sophisticated setting to enjoy handcrafted cocktails and stunning vistas.

The city's laneways are also home to numerous hidden cocktail bars. Fall from Grace, hidden beneath an unassuming sandwich shop on Collins Street, exudes an old-world charm and offers an extensive selection of expertly crafted cocktails. Eau de Vie, located down

Malthouse Lane, is known for its speakeasy vibe and creative concoctions.

5. Live Music and Entertainment
Melbourne's nightlife extends beyond dining and bars, offering a vibrant live music and

entertainment scene. The city is renowned for its thriving music venues, where you can catch local bands, international acts, and everything in between. The Corner Hotel in Richmond, The Forum in the city center, and Cherry Bar in AC/DC Lane are iconic venues that have played host to some of the world's most renowned musicians.

If you're looking for a night of laughter, Melbourne's comedy clubs are a must-visit. The Comics Lounge in North Melbourne and The Comedy Theatre in the city center regularly showcase both local and international comedians, promising a night of side-splitting humor.

Melbourne's dining and nightlife scene is a true reflection of its vibrant and diverse culture. From hidden laneway eateries and iconic fine dining establishments to rooftop bars and live music venues, the city offers an incredible range of experiences for food enthusiasts and night owls alike. Whether you're seeking a culinary adventure, a trendy bar, or a lively entertainment venue, Melbourne is sure to captivate your senses and leave a lasting impression. Explore the city's gastronomic delights and immerse yourself in the buzzing nightlife for an unforgettable experience in Australia's cultural capital.

• *Shopping in Melbourne*

Melbourne, the vibrant and cosmopolitan capital of Victoria, Australia, is renowned for its diverse culture, stunning architecture, and thriving shopping scene. Whether you're a fashionista seeking the latest trends, a food lover hunting for gourmet delights, or an art enthusiast looking for unique finds, Melbourne offers a plethora of shopping opportunities. In this comprehensive travel guide, we will explore the best shopping destinations, hidden gems, and insider tips to ensure you make the most of your shopping experience in Melbourne.

1. Iconic Shopping Precincts:

Melbourne boasts several iconic shopping precincts, each with its own distinct character and offerings. Here are some must-visit destinations:

a) Bourke Street Mall: Located in the heart of the city, Bourke Street Mall is Melbourne's premier shopping strip. It features a range of department stores, fashion boutiques, and flagship stores of renowned international brands.

b) Collins Street: Known as the "Paris End" of Melbourne, Collins Street exudes sophistication and luxury. Here, you'll find high-end fashion labels, exquisite jewelry stores, and upscale boutiques.

c) Chapel Street: Renowned for its trendy and eclectic vibe, Chapel Street is a haven for fashion-forward individuals. This vibrant precinct houses a mix of designer boutiques, vintage stores, and independent fashion labels.

d) Melbourne Central: Situated beneath the iconic shot tower, Melbourne Central is a shopping center with a twist. It combines popular fashion brands with unique specialty stores, offering a diverse retail experience.

2. Hidden Gems and Local Markets:
Beyond the mainstream shopping precincts, Melbourne is teeming with hidden gems and local markets that are worth exploring. These spots offer a blend of creativity, local craftsmanship, and a unique shopping atmosphere. Here are a few notable mentions:

a) Queen Victoria Market: Established in the 19th century, the Queen Victoria Market is an iconic Melbourne landmark. This bustling market offers an extensive range of fresh produce, gourmet delicacies, clothing, arts and crafts, and much more. Don't miss the Night Market for a lively evening of food, live music, and entertainment.

b) Degraves Street and Centre Place: Tucked away in Melbourne's laneways, Degraves Street and Centre Place are renowned for their vibrant atmosphere and thriving café culture. These narrow lanes are lined with boutique shops, quaint bookstores, and unique fashion boutiques, making them perfect for a leisurely shopping stroll.

c) Fitzroy: Located just north of the city center, Fitzroy is a bohemian neighborhood known for its artistic flair and alternative shopping scene. Explore Brunswick Street and Smith Street to discover a treasure trove of vintage clothing stores, record shops, and independent art galleries.

3. Designer Fashion and High-End Shopping:

Melbourne attracts fashion enthusiasts from around the world with its diverse range of designer fashion and high-end shopping options. The following destinations cater to those seeking luxury and sophistication:

a) Emporium Melbourne: Situated in the heart of the city, Emporium Melbourne is a premier shopping destination housing an impressive collection of local and international designer brands. It offers a seamless blend of fashion, beauty, and lifestyle experiences.

b) Chadstone - The Fashion Capital: Located a short distance from the city, Chadstone is the largest shopping center in the Southern Hemisphere. With over 500 stores, including luxury fashion houses and high-street brands, it is a paradise for fashion lovers.

c) High Street, Armadale: Nestled in the elegant suburb of Armadale, High Street boasts a selection of high-end fashion boutiques, designer labels, and stylish homeware stores. It's the perfect place to indulge in luxury shopping and experience Melbourne's affluent lifestyle.

4. *Unique and Artisanal Shopping Experiences:*

Melbourne is a hub of creativity and craftsmanship, offering a plethora of unique and artisanal shopping experiences. Here are a few recommendations:

a) Gertrude Street, Fitzroy: Gertrude Street is a mecca for art enthusiasts and lovers of independent design. Discover a range of avant-garde fashion, contemporary art galleries, and specialty stores showcasing local craftsmanship.

b) The Rose Street Artists' Market: This vibrant market in Fitzroy showcases the works of emerging artists and designers. Browse through handmade jewelry, artworks, clothing, and homeware, all while engaging with the talented creators themselves.

c) Craft Markets: Melbourne hosts various craft markets throughout the year, including the Finders Keepers Market and the Melbourne Design Market. These markets bring together local artisans and designers, offering a unique selection of handmade products, art, and design.

5. *Insider Tips and Practical Information:*

To ensure a seamless shopping experience in Melbourne, consider the following insider tips:

a) Public Transport: Utilize Melbourne's extensive tram network or the free City Circle tram to navigate the city and easily access shopping precincts.

b) Sales and Events: Keep an eye out for major sales events, such as the Melbourne Fashion Festival and the Boxing Day sales, for great deals and discounts.

c) Tax Refunds: International visitors may be eligible for a tax refund on goods purchased. Look for stores displaying the "TRS" (Tourist Refund Scheme) logo and keep your receipts handy.

d) Store Opening Hours: Most stores in Melbourne operate from 9:00 am to 5:30 pm on weekdays, with extended trading hours on Thursdays and Fridays. On weekends, trading hours may vary, so check in advance.

Melbourne's shopping scene offers an enticing blend of mainstream retail therapy, hidden gems, and unique artisanal experiences. Whether you're seeking high-end fashion, local craftsmanship, or simply immersing yourself in the city's vibrant atmosphere, Melbourne has something to offer every shopper. So, grab your shopping bags and get ready to embark on a memorable shopping adventure in the fashion capital of Australia!

• Day Trips from Melbourne

Melbourne, the vibrant capital of Victoria, Australia, is renowned for its arts and culture scene, culinary delights, and a plethora of tourist attractions. However, beyond the city's bustling streets lies a world of natural wonders waiting to be discovered. This travel guide will take you on a journey through the best day trips from Melbourne, showcasing the diverse landscapes, stunning coastlines, charming towns, and unique wildlife encounters that await just a short distance from the city.

1. The Great Ocean Road
No visit to Melbourne is complete without embarking on a day trip along the iconic Great Ocean Road. This 243-kilometer stretch of breathtaking coastline offers a stunning mix of

rugged cliffs, golden beaches, and ancient rainforests. Highlights along the way include the famous Twelve Apostles, Loch Ard Gorge, and the picturesque seaside town of Lorne. Travelers can enjoy panoramic views, go surfing, spot wildlife, and immerse themselves in the region's rich history.

2. Phillip Island

Located just 90 minutes from Melbourne, Phillip Island is a haven for wildlife enthusiasts. The island is renowned for its adorable little penguins, which can be observed returning to shore in the evening during the popular Penguin Parade. Additionally, visitors can witness seals basking at Seal Rocks, explore the Koala Conservation Centre, and enjoy the island's beautiful beaches. Motorsports enthusiasts should not miss the chance to watch the thrilling Australian Motorcycle Grand Prix held at the Phillip Island Grand Prix Circuit.

3. The Yarra Valley

For wine connoisseurs and food lovers, a day trip to the Yarra Valley is a must. Situated less than an hour from Melbourne, this picturesque region is known for its vineyards, wineries, and gourmet delights. Visitors can indulge in wine tastings at renowned estates, savor farm-to-table cuisine at local restaurants, and explore charming towns like Healesville. The Yarra Valley also offers opportunities for hot air balloon rides, scenic drives, and visits to the Healesville Sanctuary, where native Australian wildlife can be admired up close.

4. The Mornington Peninsula

The Mornington Peninsula, just an hour's drive from Melbourne, is a diverse playground of natural beauty, coastal charm, and wellness experiences. Visitors can soak in hot springs, stroll along pristine beaches, explore coastal trails, and indulge in local produce at the peninsula's renowned wineries and farm gates. The region is also home to the famous Cape Schanck Lighthouse, the picturesque seaside village of Sorrento, and the iconic bathing boxes at Brighton Beach.

5. Wilsons Promontory National Park

A bit further from Melbourne, but well worth the trip, Wilsons Promontory National Park offers a pristine wilderness experience. Known affectionately as "The Prom" by locals, this coastal paradise boasts stunning beaches, lush forests, and abundant wildlife. Hiking enthusiasts can explore numerous trails, including the popular hike to the summit of Mount Oberon for panoramic views. Wildlife encounters are common here, with opportunities to spot kangaroos, wombats, emus, and a variety of bird species. Camping and beachside accommodation options are available for those who want to immerse themselves in the park's natural beauty.

Melbourne's strategic location provides an array of remarkable day trip options, allowing visitors to escape the city and explore the diverse landscapes of Victoria. Whether it's the breathtaking Great Ocean Road, the wildlife haven of Phillip Island, the picturesque Yarra Valley, the coastal beauty of the Mornington Peninsula, or the pristine wilderness of Wilsons Promontory National Park, these day trips promise unforgettable experiences and a deeper appreciation for the natural wonders that surround Melbourne. So, pack your bags, embark on these adventures, and create lifelong memories in Australia's captivating landscapes.

CHAPTER FIVE

Great Barrier Reef

•*Overview of the Great Barrier Reef*

Australia is home to some of the world's most spectacular natural wonders, and none are more iconic than the Great Barrier Reef. Located off the northeastern coast of the country, this vast coral reef ecosystem is a UNESCO World Heritage Site and a must-visit destination for nature enthusiasts and adventure seekers alike. Stretching over 2,300 kilometers (1,400 miles), the Great Barrier Reef is the largest coral reef system on the planet, teeming with breathtaking marine life and offering unparalleled opportunities for snorkeling, diving, and exploration. In this Australia travel guide, we will provide a comprehensive overview of the Great Barrier Reef, including its natural features, ecological significance, and the best ways to experience this magnificent wonder.

1. Natural Features of the Great Barrier Reef

The Great Barrier Reef is a marvel of nature, composed of nearly 3,000 individual coral reefs and around 900 islands. It spans an area of approximately 344,400 square kilometers (133,000 square miles) and can be seen from space. The reef system is made up of both hard and soft corals, which provide a diverse and colorful underwater landscape. These corals create a complex habitat for a vast array of marine species, including more than 1,500 species of fish, 30 species of whales and dolphins, six species of sea turtles, and countless other marine creatures.

The reef itself is divided into various regions, each with its unique features. The northern section, known as the Ribbon Reefs, is renowned for its vibrant corals and is a popular spot for diving and snorkeling. Further south, the Whitsunday Islands offer picturesque beaches and stunning turquoise waters, with the iconic Heart Reef being a highlight. The southern section of the reef, off the coast of Cairns, is easily accessible and offers excellent diving opportunities, including exploring the famous Cod Hole and the Ribbon Reefs.

2. Ecological Significance and Conservation

The Great Barrier Reef is not only a visual spectacle but also a critical ecosystem that supports an incredible diversity of marine life. It is home to numerous endangered species and serves as a breeding ground for many migratory birds and marine creatures. The reef's ecological significance extends beyond its borders, as it plays a crucial role in maintaining oceanic and climatic balance.

However, the Great Barrier Reef faces various environmental challenges, including coral bleaching caused by rising sea temperatures, pollution, overfishing, and crown-of-thorns starfish outbreaks. To protect this natural treasure, extensive conservation efforts are underway. The Australian government, in collaboration with research institutions and local communities, has implemented initiatives to reduce pollution, regulate fishing practices, and monitor the health of the reef. Visitors are encouraged to practice responsible tourism by following guidelines to minimize their impact on the fragile ecosystem.

3. Experiencing the Great Barrier Reef

A trip to Australia would be incomplete without exploring the wonders of the Great Barrier Reef. There are several ways to experience this natural marvel, catering to a wide range of interests and preferences.

a) Snorkeling and Diving: The reef's crystal-clear waters provide excellent visibility, making snorkeling and diving incredibly popular activities. Whether you are a novice or an experienced diver, there are options for everyone. Cairns and the Whitsunday Islands are popular starting points for diving excursions, with certified instructors and dive operators available to guide you through the underwater wonders. Snorkeling trips are also readily available, allowing you to witness the colorful coral formations and swim alongside tropical fish.

b) Island Exploration: The Great Barrier Reef is dotted with numerous islands, each offering unique experiences. Hamilton Island and Lizard Island are well-known tourist destinations, providing luxurious accommodations, pristine

beaches, and access to a range of water sports. Green Island and Fitzroy Island, located close to Cairns, are easily accessible and offer excellent snorkeling opportunities.

c) Cruises and Boat Tours: A variety of cruise options are available for those who prefer a more relaxed approach to exploring the Great Barrier Reef. From day trips to multi-day excursions, these cruises offer the chance to witness the reef's beauty from the comfort of a boat, with onboard amenities and knowledgeable guides to enhance your experience. Some cruises even include activities such as helicopter rides, underwater observatories, and guided nature walks on the islands.

d) Aerial Perspectives: For a truly awe-inspiring view of the Great Barrier Reef, consider taking a scenic flight or helicopter tour. From above, you can appreciate the sheer size and intricate patterns of the reef, as well as spot marine life and enjoy breathtaking panoramas of the surrounding ocean and islands.

The Great Barrier Reef is an unparalleled natural wonder that captivates the imagination and leaves visitors in awe of its beauty and biodiversity. As a UNESCO World Heritage

Site, it holds immense ecological significance and is a testament to Australia's commitment to environmental preservation. Whether you choose to snorkel, dive, cruise, or simply soak in the panoramic views, exploring the Great Barrier Reef is an experience that will stay with you forever.

As you plan your Australian adventure, be sure to prioritize a visit to the Great Barrier Reef. Embrace the opportunity to witness this remarkable ecosystem firsthand and contribute to its conservation through responsible tourism practices. With its stunning coral formations, vibrant marine life, and endless opportunities for exploration, the Great Barrier Reef promises an unforgettable journey into the heart of Australia's natural wonders.

• *Exploring the Reef*

Australia is a land of natural wonders, and one of its most extraordinary treasures is the Great Barrier Reef. Stretching over 2,300 kilometers along the Queensland coast, this majestic underwater ecosystem is a UNESCO World Heritage site and one of the seven wonders of the natural world. In this comprehensive Australia travel guide, we will delve into the mesmerizing realm of the Great Barrier Reef, offering insights on the best ways to explore and experience this breathtaking wonderland.

1. Understanding the Great Barrier Reef:

The Great Barrier Reef is a vibrant and diverse ecosystem consisting of over 2,900 individual reefs and 900 islands. It is home to an incredible array of marine life, including 1,500 species of fish, 600 types of coral, and numerous other fascinating creatures. Before embarking on your journey, learn about the reef's importance, its delicate ecosystem, and the conservation efforts in place to protect this natural wonder for future generations.

2. Best Time to Visit:

Australia's tropical climate influences the best time to explore the Great Barrier Reef. The months between June and October offer excellent weather conditions with warm temperatures and reduced rainfall. During this period, the water visibility is usually at its best, making it ideal for diving and snorkeling adventures.

3. Gateway to the Reef: Cairns:

Cairns, located in Far North Queensland, is the most popular gateway to the Great Barrier Reef. This vibrant coastal city offers a plethora of accommodation options, tour operators, and easy access to the reef. Explore the Cairns Esplanade, visit the Cairns Aquarium, and discover the city's rich Indigenous culture before diving into the underwater paradise.

4. Snorkeling: Exploring the Shallow Depths:

Snorkeling is the perfect way to discover the vibrant coral gardens and abundant marine life of the Great Barrier Reef. Whether you are a beginner or an experienced snorkeler, there are numerous spots suitable for all skill levels. From the Low Isles near Port Douglas to the famous Agincourt Reef, immerse yourself in the captivating world beneath the surface.

5. Scuba Diving: Delving into the Depths:

For those seeking a more immersive experience, scuba diving in the Great Barrier Reef offers unparalleled encounters with marine life and stunning coral formations. Certified divers can explore renowned dive sites such as the Cod Hole, Osprey Reef, and the Ribbon Reefs. Novices can also participate in introductory dives under the guidance of experienced instructors.

6. Sailing and Cruising Adventures:
Another enchanting way to explore the Great Barrier Reef is by embarking on a sailing or cruising adventure. Hop aboard a luxury yacht, a catamaran, or a traditional schooner and set sail on the turquoise waters. Enjoy snorkeling, diving, and relaxing on secluded beaches, all while indulging in delectable meals and breathtaking views.

7. Island Escapes: Exploring the Whitsundays:
The Whitsunday Islands, situated within the Great Barrier Reef, offer a paradise of pristine beaches, crystal-clear waters, and lush rainforests. Popular among travelers, the Whitsundays is an ideal destination for island hopping, where you can explore famous spots like Whitehaven Beach, Hamilton Island, and Daydream Island.

8. Marine Wildlife Encounters:
Encountering the magnificent marine wildlife is an unforgettable experience in the Great Barrier Reef. Keep an eye out for majestic

humpback whales during their migration season, witness the playful dolphins, and observe the gentle sea turtles that call the reef home. Several tour operators offer dedicated wildlife experiences, ensuring you have the chance to witness these incredible creatures up close.

9. Conservation and Responsible Tourism:

Preserving the Great Barrier Reef is of utmost importance. Learn about sustainable practices,

support responsible tour operators, and be mindful of your actions while exploring the reef. Several organizations and research centers offer educational programs, allowing visitors to contribute to ongoing conservation efforts.

10. Beyond the Reef: Explore the Surrounding Attractions:

While the Great Barrier Reef steals the spotlight, there are numerous other attractions to explore in the region. Discover the Daintree Rainforest, the world's oldest tropical rainforest, visit the vibrant city of Brisbane, or venture inland to experience the ancient wonders of the Australian Outback.

Exploring the Great Barrier Reef is a dream come true for nature enthusiasts and adventure seekers alike. With its remarkable marine biodiversity, stunning coral formations, and picturesque islands, this underwater wonderland promises an unforgettable journey. By following this Australia travel guide, you will be well-equipped to embark on an extraordinary adventure to one of the world's most remarkable natural treasures. Remember to respect and protect the reef, leaving only footprints and taking away memories that will last a lifetime.

Snorkeling and Diving

Australia is renowned for its breathtaking underwater wonders, offering unparalleled opportunities for snorkeling and diving enthusiasts. With its extensive coastline, vibrant coral reefs, diverse marine life, and crystal-clear waters, Australia is a true paradise for those seeking to explore the underwater realm. This travel guide aims to provide an in-depth overview of the top snorkeling and diving destinations in Australia, along with essential information to ensure a memorable and safe experience.

1. *The Great Barrier Reef:*

No discussion about snorkeling and diving in Australia would be complete without mentioning the Great Barrier Reef. This natural wonder stretches over 2,300 kilometers, making it the largest coral reef system in the world. With its kaleidoscope of colors, intricate coral formations, and an abundance of marine species, the Great Barrier Reef is a must-visit destination for any diving or snorkeling enthusiast. From Cairns and Port Douglas, visitors can embark on diving and snorkeling tours to explore this UNESCO World Heritage site and encounter mesmerizing marine creatures such as turtles, reef sharks, and vibrant tropical fish.

2. *Ningaloo Reef:*

Located off the coast of Western Australia, Ningaloo Reef is another spectacular destination for underwater exploration. What sets Ningaloo Reef apart is its accessibility from the shore, making it ideal for snorkelers and divers of all skill levels. The reef is renowned for its annual whale shark migration, where lucky visitors can swim alongside these gentle giants. Snorkelers can also encounter manta rays, humpback whales, and an array of colorful fish and coral species. Coral Bay and Exmouth are the main towns offering access to Ningaloo Reef, with various tour operators providing guided experiences.

3. The Whitsunday Islands:
Situated in the heart of the Great Barrier Reef, the Whitsunday Islands offer a unique blend of pristine beaches and remarkable diving opportunities. Renowned sites such as the Great Barrier Reef Marine Park and the famous Bait Reef provide divers with the chance to explore vibrant coral gardens, swim among reef sharks and stingrays, and witness the stunning underwater diversity. Snorkelers can also enjoy shallow reefs teeming with marine life, or simply relax on the idyllic beaches that dot the islands.

4. Lord Howe Island:
Listed as a UNESCO World Heritage site, Lord Howe Island is a hidden gem located off the coast of New South Wales. Its protected marine park is a paradise for snorkelers and divers, boasting crystal-clear waters, diverse coral formations, and an array of endemic species. Snorkelers can glide over vibrant coral gardens,

encountering turtles, colorful reef fish, and even the rare Lord Howe Island stick insect. Divers can explore impressive drop-offs, underwater caves, and the world-famous Ball's Pyramid, a volcanic formation rising dramatically from the ocean.

5. The Coral Sea:

For experienced divers seeking adventure, the Coral Sea offers unparalleled opportunities. This remote region, located northeast of Australia, is home to pristine reefs, abundant pelagic species, and remarkable dive sites such as Osprey Reef and Holmes Reef. Here, divers can encounter sharks, massive schools of fish, and even dive with dwarf minke whales during their annual migration. Liveaboard expeditions depart from Cairns and provide multi-day diving trips to explore the wonders of the Coral Sea.

Safety Tips:

- Ensure you have the necessary snorkeling or diving certification before embarking on underwater activities.
- Always dive or snorkel with a buddy and follow the instructions of your guide or instructor.

- Be mindful of the marine environment and avoid touching or damaging coral and marine life.
- Check the weather conditions and visibility before diving or snorkeling.
- Use reef-safe sunscreen to protect the delicate ecosystems.
- Stay hydrated
  and practice proper dive safety protocols, including surface intervals and dive planning.

Australia offers an array of unparalleled snorkeling and diving experiences that cater to both beginners and seasoned underwater adventurers. From the iconic Great Barrier Reef to the remote Coral Sea, the country's diverse marine ecosystems and pristine waters provide endless opportunities for exploration. Whether you prefer to snorkel along vibrant coral reefs or embark on thrilling dives into the depths of the ocean, Australia's underwater wonders will leave you with memories to last a lifetime. So, pack your gear, immerse yourself in the aquatic realm, and get ready for an extraordinary adventure Down Under.

Boat Tours and Cruises

Australia, a land of stunning coastlines, vibrant marine life, and breathtaking natural wonders, offers a multitude of opportunities for exploring its waters through boat tours and cruises. From sailing along the Great Barrier Reef, the world's largest coral reef system, to navigating the serene waters of Sydney Harbour, these experiences provide an immersive way to discover the country's diverse ecosystems and iconic landmarks. In this Australia travel guide, we will delve into the captivating world of boat tours and cruises, highlighting the top destinations and the unique experiences they offer.

1. Sydney Harbour:

The sparkling blue waters of Sydney Harbour serve as the backdrop for one of Australia's most iconic boat tour experiences. Hop aboard a luxury yacht or join a guided cruise to witness the magnificent Sydney Opera House and the Harbour Bridge from a unique vantage point. Explore secluded bays, visit picturesque islands, and soak in the breathtaking views of the city's skyline. Don't miss the chance to witness the famous New Year's Eve fireworks extravaganza or embark on a sunset dinner cruise for a truly memorable experience.

2. Great Barrier Reef:

The Great Barrier Reef, a UNESCO World Heritage Site, is a must-visit destination for nature enthusiasts. Embark on a boat tour from Cairns, Port Douglas, or Airlie Beach, and prepare to be amazed by the vibrant coral gardens and an array of marine life. Snorkeling or diving in these pristine waters provides an up-close encounter with tropical fish, turtles, and even reef sharks. For a more leisurely experience, choose a multi-day cruise that combines diving, snorkeling, and relaxation, allowing you to explore multiple sections of this vast ecosystem.

3. Whitsunday Islands:

Located in the heart of the Great Barrier Reef, the Whitsunday Islands offer a unique blend of pristine beaches, secluded coves, and crystal-clear waters. Join a sailing tour or hop aboard a catamaran to explore the 74 islands that make up this tropical paradise. Don't miss the iconic Whitehaven Beach, known for its pure white silica sand and turquoise waters. Snorkel or dive in the Great Barrier Reef's outer fringes, explore secluded anchorages, and enjoy the tranquility of this breathtaking archipelago.

4. Kimberley Coast:

For an off-the-beaten-path adventure, head to Western Australia's Kimberley Coast. This remote and rugged region is best explored by boat, allowing you to navigate the winding rivers, towering cliffs, and ancient gorges that define its landscape. Marvel at the Horizontal Falls, a natural wonder where tidal currents rush through narrow gorges, creating a thrilling spectacle. Encounter majestic waterfalls, indigenous rock art, and abundant wildlife, including crocodiles and sea turtles. A Kimberley Coast cruise promises a unique and awe-inspiring experience.

5. Murray River:

In the heart of Australia, the mighty Murray River meanders through picturesque landscapes, offering a serene and relaxing boating experience. Join a paddle steamer cruise or hire a houseboat to navigate the tranquil waters flanked by red gum forests and charming riverside towns. Immerse yourself in the region's rich history, explore vineyards, and indulge in local produce. Whether it's a short day trip or a leisurely week-long cruise, the Murray River provides a delightful escape from bustling city life.

6. Tasmania's Wilderness:

Tasmania, an island state located south of the mainland, boasts pristine wilderness and rugged coastlines. Embark on a boat tour along the Tasman Peninsula to witness the towering sea cliffs of the Tasman National Park, including the iconic formations of the Three Capes. Explore the remote Southwest National Park, accessible only by boat or plane, to discover untouched landscapes, dramatic fjords, and abundant wildlife. From spotting seals and dolphins to encountering albatrosses and penguins, Tasmania's boat tours offer an immersive exploration of its natural wonders.

Australia's boat tours and cruises provide a gateway to the country's remarkable aquatic landscapes, allowing visitors to connect with nature, discover hidden gems, and create lasting memories. Whether it's the colorful coral reefs of the Great Barrier Reef, the captivating Sydney Harbour, or the remote wilderness of Tasmania, each destination offers a unique and unforgettable experience. So, set sail, embrace the sea breeze, and embark on an incredible journey through Australia's breathtaking waters.

Island Resorts

Australia, with its stunning coastline and diverse natural beauty, is home to several captivating island resorts. These idyllic retreats offer a perfect blend of luxury, adventure, and relaxation. From the Great Barrier Reef to the picturesque Whitsunday Islands, this travel guide will take you on a virtual tour of some of the most enchanting island resorts in Australia.

1. Hamilton Island:

Located in the heart of the Whitsundays, Hamilton Island is a popular choice for travelers seeking a luxurious island escape. The island boasts pristine white-sand beaches, crystal-clear waters, and lush tropical landscapes. The luxurious accommodation options, such as the iconic Qualia Resort, offer breathtaking views and world-class amenities. Visitors can indulge in a range of activities including snorkeling, sailing, and exploring the Great Barrier Reef.

2. Hayman Island:

Renowned for its exclusivity and natural beauty, Hayman Island is another gem in the Whitsundays. Following an extensive renovation, the InterContinental Hayman Island Resort now stands as a premier destination for luxury travelers. With its private beach, exquisite dining options, and rejuvenating spa experiences, this island resort provides the ultimate indulgence. Visitors can also enjoy various water sports, helicopter tours, and guided hikes through the island's rugged terrain.

3. Lizard Island:
Located on the Great Barrier Reef, Lizard Island offers a secluded and pristine getaway for nature enthusiasts. The resort on this island provides an intimate and luxurious experience, with only 40 suites available. Guests can explore the underwater wonders of the Great Barrier Reef through snorkeling or scuba diving, embark on guided nature walks, or simply relax on the island's secluded beaches. Lizard Island is truly a paradise for those seeking tranquility and natural beauty.

4. Orpheus Island:
For a secluded and intimate retreat, Orpheus Island is an ideal choice. This island resort is situated amidst the Great Barrier Reef and offers exclusive access to some of the world's most vibrant coral gardens. With just a handful of rooms and suites, Orpheus Island Lodge provides an intimate and personalized

experience. Guests can partake in snorkeling, fishing, and kayaking, or enjoy a gourmet picnic on a private beach. The resort's focus on sustainability and conservation adds to its allure.

5. Bedarra Island:
Tucked away in the Great Barrier Reef Marine Park, Bedarra Island is a haven of luxury and seclusion. With only ten private villas nestled amidst lush rainforest and offering breathtaking ocean views, this resort ensures an exclusive and intimate experience. Visitors can indulge in spa treatments, explore secluded beaches, and enjoy gourmet dining experiences. Bedarra Island is a perfect choice for couples seeking a romantic escape or anyone yearning for a serene and tranquil environment.

Australia's island resorts offer a slice of paradise for travelers seeking luxury, adventure, and natural beauty. From the world-famous Whitsundays to the Great Barrier Reef islands, each destination presents a unique and unforgettable experience. Whether you prefer lounging on pristine beaches, exploring vibrant coral reefs, or immersing yourself in lush rainforests, the island resorts in Australia cater to a wide range of interests. These idyllic retreats promise a perfect blend of relaxation, adventure, and indulgence, making them a must-visit for any traveler exploring the wonders of Australia.

• *Marine Life and Conservation*

Melbourne, the vibrant coastal city of Australia, not only boasts a rich cultural heritage and bustling urban life but also offers incredible opportunities to explore and appreciate the beauty of marine life. With its stunning coastline, diverse marine ecosystems, and commitment to conservation efforts, Melbourne is a dream destination for nature enthusiasts and ocean lovers alike. This travel guide aims to showcase the marine wonders of Melbourne and highlight the importance of conservation to preserve this delicate ecosystem for future generations.

1. The Marine Biodiversity of Melbourne:

Melbourne's coastal waters are home to a wide array of marine species, making it a haven for marine biologists and nature enthusiasts. The Port Phillip Bay, located just a stone's throw away from the city, is a thriving marine ecosystem teeming with vibrant corals, seagrass beds, and an abundance of marine life. From colorful tropical fish to majestic dolphins and seals, the diversity of marine species in this region is awe-inspiring.

2. *Exploring Marine Parks and Reserves:*

To experience the best of Melbourne's marine life, exploring the various marine parks and reserves is a must. The Port Phillip Heads Marine National Park, located at the entrance of Port Phillip Bay, offers exceptional diving and snorkeling opportunities, allowing visitors to witness the underwater wonders up close. Here, you can encounter magnificent kelp forests, seahorses, stingrays, and even the elusive Weedy Seadragon.

3. *Wildlife Encounters:*

Melbourne's waters provide ample opportunities to interact with marine wildlife. The coastal regions are frequented by dolphins, especially in Port Phillip Bay, where you can embark on a guided dolphin-watching tour. These intelligent creatures often swim alongside boats, providing an unforgettable experience. Additionally, seal colonies can be spotted in areas like Chinaman's Hat and

Pope's Eye, offering a chance to observe these playful creatures in their natural habitat.

4. Sustainable Tourism and Conservation Efforts:

As visitors, it is crucial to appreciate the marine environment responsibly and contribute to its conservation. Melbourne takes pride in its sustainable tourism practices and initiatives aimed at protecting marine ecosystems. Several organizations and research institutions in the region are actively involved in conservation projects, such as seagrass restoration, marine debris cleanup, and protecting endangered species. Travelers can support these efforts by choosing eco-friendly tour operators, following responsible diving and snorkeling practices, and participating in volunteer programs.

5. Marine Education and Awareness Centers:

To deepen your understanding of marine life and conservation, a visit to Melbourne's marine education and awareness centers is highly recommended. The Melbourne Aquarium, located in the heart of the city, offers an immersive experience with its vast collection of marine species and interactive exhibits. It also conducts educational programs on marine conservation, raising awareness among visitors of all ages. Another notable attraction is the Marine and Freshwater Discovery Centre in Queenscliff, where visitors can learn about marine research, participate in interactive displays, and gain insights into ongoing conservation projects.

6. Sustainable Seafood and Culinary Experiences:

Melbourne's culinary scene is renowned for its delectable seafood offerings. To ensure sustainable seafood consumption, consider dining at restaurants that prioritize serving responsibly sourced fish and shellfish. Look for establishments certified by organizations such as the Marine Stewardship Council (MSC) or those committed to supporting local fisheries and implementing sustainable fishing practices. This way, you can relish the flavors of Melbourne's coastal cuisine while promoting responsible seafood consumption.

7. Beach Cleanups and Community Involvement:

Engaging in beach cleanups and community-driven conservation activities is a meaningful way to contribute to marine conservation efforts in Melbourne. Many local organizations and volunteer groups organize regular beach cleaning initiatives, inviting residents and visitors to participate. Joining such events allows you to witness firsthand the impact of marine pollution and actively contribute to keeping the coastlines clean and pristine.

Melbourne's coastal wonders and commitment to marine conservation make it an ideal destination for eco-conscious travelers. From exploring marine parks and encountering magnificent wildlife to supporting sustainable tourism practices and participating in conservation initiatives, there are numerous ways to appreciate and preserve Melbourne's marine life. By experiencing the natural beauty of this region and understanding the importance of conservation, visitors can become ambassadors for marine biodiversity and play a vital role in ensuring the long-term sustainability of Melbourne's marine ecosystems.

• *Nearby Attractions*

Melbourne, the vibrant capital city of Victoria in Australia, is renowned for its cultural diversity, stunning architecture, and thriving arts scene. While the city itself offers a plethora of attractions and activities, it also serves as a gateway to several remarkable destinations in its vicinity. In this comprehensive Australia travel guide, we will delve into the nearby attractions that await visitors in Melbourne, offering a wide range of experiences, from breathtaking natural wonders to charming coastal towns and cultural landmarks.

1. Great Ocean Road (Distance from Melbourne: Approx. 100 km):

One of Australia's most iconic road trips, the Great Ocean Road, is an absolute must-visit when exploring Melbourne. This scenic coastal drive spans approximately 243 kilometers, hugging the stunning coastline and offering breathtaking vistas of the Southern Ocean. Highlights along the route include the Twelve Apostles, a collection of limestone stacks rising from the ocean, as well as picturesque coastal towns such as Lorne and Apollo Bay. Visitors can also indulge in various outdoor activities like surfing, hiking, and wildlife spotting along the way.

2. *Phillip Island (Distance from Melbourne: Approx. 140 km):*

Located just a short drive from Melbourne, Phillip Island is a popular destination for wildlife enthusiasts. The island is home to a unique spectacle known as the Penguin Parade, where visitors can witness hundreds of little penguins returning to shore at sunset after a day of fishing. Additionally, Phillip Island offers opportunities to observe Australian fur seals at Seal Rocks, visit the Koala Conservation Centre, and enjoy stunning coastal scenery at Cape Woolamai and The Nobbies.

3. *Yarra Valley (Distance from Melbourne: Approx. 60 km):*

Wine connoisseurs and nature lovers alike will be captivated by the enchanting Yarra Valley. This renowned wine region boasts picturesque vineyards, cellar doors, and award-winning wineries. Visitors can embark on wine tasting tours, sample world-class chocolates at the Yarra Valley Chocolaterie, and savor delectable gourmet experiences at the region's fine restaurants. In addition to its wine heritage, the Yarra Valley offers opportunities for hot air ballooning, exploring the Healesville Sanctuary to encounter native Australian wildlife, and enjoying scenic walks in the Dandenong Ranges National Park.

4. Mornington Peninsula (Distance from Melbourne: Approx. 80 km):

The charming Mornington Peninsula is a haven for nature enthusiasts and beach lovers. Visitors can relax on pristine sandy shores, such as Sorrento and Rye, or take a dip in the soothing hot springs of Peninsula Hot Springs. The region is also renowned for its culinary delights, with numerous vineyards, farm gates, and restaurants offering fresh local produce and exquisite wines. Nature lovers can explore the coastal trails of Cape Schanck and Point Nepean, visit the Moonlit Sanctuary Wildlife Conservation Park, or take a scenic gondola ride at the Arthurs Seat Eagle.

5. Wilsons Promontory National Park (Distance from Melbourne: Approx. 220 km):

For those seeking a wilderness escape, Wilsons Promontory National Park is an ideal destination. Affectionately known as "The Prom," this pristine national park showcases diverse landscapes, including rugged mountains, tranquil rivers, and unspoiled beaches. Visitors can embark on scenic hikes, such as the popular Lilly Pilly Gully Circuit or the challenging Mount Oberon Summit Trail, to witness breathtaking panoramic views. Wildlife encounters are also common, with opportunities to spot kangaroos, wombats, and emus roaming freely.

Melbourne's proximity to these remarkable nearby attractions ensures that visitors have an incredible array of experiences at their fingertips. From the awe-inspiring coastal drive along the Great Ocean Road to the enchanting wildlife encounters on Phillip Island and the scenic wonders of the Yarra Valley and Mornington Peninsula, there is something for every traveler. Whether you are an outdoor enthusiast, a wildlife lover, a wine connoisseur, or simply seeking to explore the beauty of nature, these destinations near Melbourne are sure to leave a lasting impression and enrich your Australian travel experience.

CHAPTER SIX

Cairns and Tropical North Queensland

•*Overview of Cairns and Tropical North Queensland*

Nestled in the northeastern corner of Australia, Cairns and Tropical North Queensland offer a captivating blend of natural wonders, vibrant cultural experiences, and awe-inspiring landscapes. From the magnificent Barrier Reef to the ancient Daintree Rainforest, this region showcases the best of Australia's tropical paradise. This travel guide provides a comprehensive overview of Cairns and Tropical North Queensland, highlighting their unique attractions, adventurous activities, rich indigenous heritage, and delightful culinary experiences. Embark on a memorable journey through this remarkable part of Australia and discover the essence of nature's grandeur.

I. Geographical and Cultural Background

Cairns and Tropical North Queensland are located in the state of Queensland, encompassing a vast area stretching from the city of Cairns along the eastern coast to the tropical rainforests of Cape York Peninsula. The region is characterized by a tropical climate, with wet and dry seasons influencing the landscape and natural ecosystems. The area is home to the Aboriginal peoples, who have a rich cultural heritage and connection to the land.

II. Natural Wonders

1. Great Barrier Reef:

The Great Barrier Reef, a UNESCO World Heritage site, is one of the most iconic attractions in Cairns and Tropical North Queensland. Spanning over 2,300 kilometers, it is the largest coral reef system in the world, teeming with vibrant marine life. Snorkeling, scuba diving, and sailing trips offer unparalleled opportunities to explore this underwater paradise.

2. Daintree Rainforest:

Nestled north of Cairns, the Daintree Rainforest is one of the oldest surviving rainforests on the planet, dating back 180 million years. Its lush greenery, cascading waterfalls, and diverse wildlife make it a nature lover's paradise. Take a guided tour, hike through the ancient trails, or go bird-watching to immerse yourself in this captivating ecosystem.

3. Atherton Tablelands:
Located southwest of Cairns, the Atherton Tablelands is a fertile plateau adorned with rolling hills, waterfalls, and picturesque lakes. It offers opportunities for wildlife spotting, exploring the quaint villages, and indulging in the region's renowned food and wine trails.

III. Adventurous Activities

1. Scenic Helicopter Flights:
Experience breathtaking aerial views of the Great Barrier Reef, Daintree Rainforest, and the region's stunning coastline with a thrilling helicopter ride. Capture the beauty of the landscape from above and create memories that will last a lifetime.

2. White Water Rafting:
For adventure enthusiasts, the Tully and Barron Rivers present thrilling white water rafting experiences. Navigate through rapids,

enjoy the rush of adrenaline, and witness the beauty of the surrounding rainforest as you conquer the untamed waters.

3. Hot Air Ballooning:
Gently ascend into the sky at sunrise and witness the panoramic vistas of Cairns and Tropical North Queensland from a hot air balloon. Drift above the Atherton Tablelands or Mareeba Valley, marveling at the patchwork of lush green fields and volcanic craters.

4. Rainforest Zip-lining:
Zip-lining through the rainforest canopy offers a unique perspective of the lush landscape. Soar above the treetops, experiencing an exhilarating adventure while learning about the region's diverse flora and fauna from knowledgeable guides.

IV. Indigenous Heritage and Cultural Experiences
1. Tjapukai Aboriginal Cultural Park:
At Tjapukai, you can immerse yourself in the rich indigenous heritage of the region. Engage in interactive cultural performances, learn traditional arts and crafts, and savor authentic indigenous cuisine.

2. Mossman G

orge:
Explore the Mossman Gorge, a significant
cultural site for the local Kuku Yalanji people.
Take a guided Dreamtime Walk, where
indigenous guides share stories, traditions, and
the medicinal properties of the rainforest
plants.

3. Aboriginal Art:
Discover the vibrant Aboriginal art scene in
Cairns and Tropical North Queensland. Visit
local galleries to admire intricate dot paintings,
traditional artifacts, and contemporary works
that showcase the indigenous culture's deep
connection with the land.

V. Culinary Delights
Cairns and Tropical North Queensland boast a
diverse culinary scene that reflects the region's
tropical flavors and multicultural influences.
From fresh seafood to tropical fruits, here are
some culinary highlights:

1. Seafood:
Indulge in an array of fresh seafood delicacies,
including mud crabs, prawns, barramundi, and
coral trout. Taste the catch of the day at

waterfront restaurants or savor a seafood platter while enjoying breathtaking ocean views.

2. Tropical Fruits:
Sample an abundance of tropical fruits, such as mangoes, papayas, lychees, and passionfruit. Visit local markets, like Rusty's Market in Cairns, to experience the vibrant colors, flavors, and aromas of the region's produce.

3. Indigenous Cuisine:
Discover the unique flavors of indigenous cuisine by trying traditional dishes like kangaroo, crocodile, and bush tucker ingredients. Join a bush food tour to learn about the native ingredients and their cultural significance.

Cairns and Tropical North Queensland offer an extraordinary travel experience with their breathtaking natural wonders, adventurous activities, indigenous heritage, and delightful cuisine. Whether you seek relaxation, exploration, or a cultural immersion, this region has something to captivate every traveler. Immerse yourself in the wonders of the Great Barrier Reef, lose yourself in the ancient rainforests, and connect with the rich indigenous culture. Cairns and Tropical North Queensland beckon adventurers and nature enthusiasts to embark on a remarkable journey through Australia's tropical paradise.

• *Top Attractions*

Nestled in the northeastern corner of Australia, Cairns and Tropical North Queensland offer a captivating blend of natural wonders, cultural heritage, and adrenaline-pumping adventures. Boasting pristine beaches, lush rainforests, and the iconic Great Barrier Reef, this region is a haven for nature enthusiasts and adventure seekers alike. In this Australia travel guide, we will delve into the top attractions of Cairns and Tropical North Queensland, providing an in-depth exploration of the region's most enchanting destinations.

1. *Great Barrier Reef:*
Undoubtedly one of the world's most remarkable natural wonders, the Great Barrier Reef is a must-visit attraction for anyone traveling to Cairns and Tropical North Queensland. This UNESCO World Heritage Site stretches over 2,300 kilometers (1,400 miles) and is home to a staggering array of

marine life. Embark on a snorkeling or scuba diving expedition to witness the vibrant coral gardens, swim alongside tropical fish, and marvel at the majestic manta rays and sea turtles. For those who prefer to stay dry, take a scenic helicopter or boat tour to appreciate the sheer magnitude of this magnificent ecosystem.

2. Daintree Rainforest:
Escape into the heart of nature at the Daintree Rainforest, the oldest tropical rainforest on Earth. As you wander through this ancient wilderness, you'll encounter an abundance of flora and fauna, including unique bird species, lush ferns, and towering trees. Take a guided tour to explore the diverse ecosystems, trek through the Mossman Gorge, or cruise along the Daintree River to spot crocodiles in their natural habitat. Don't miss the opportunity to visit Cape Tribulation, where the rainforest meets the Great Barrier Reef, creating a truly awe-inspiring landscape.

3. Kuranda Village:
Nestled amidst the rainforest, Kuranda Village offers a delightful blend of nature, arts, and culture. Reach this charming village by scenic rail journey on the Kuranda Scenic Railway or glide above the treetops on the Skyrail

Rainforest Cableway. Once in Kuranda, explore the vibrant markets filled with local handicrafts, indulge in delicious cuisine at the various eateries, and visit the Australian Butterfly Sanctuary. For a unique experience, interact with native wildlife at the Kuranda Koala Gardens and Birdworld Kuranda, where you can cuddle a koala or hand-feed colorful lorikeets.

4. Cape Tribulation:

Venture to Cape Tribulation, a captivating destination where two UNESCO World Heritage sites converge—the Daintree Rainforest and the Great Barrier Reef. Relax on pristine beaches, go horseback riding along the shore, or hike through the rainforest on well-marked trails. Join a guided night tour to witness the enchanting spectacle of bioluminescent creatures illuminating the shoreline. Cape Tribulation offers a secluded and idyllic getaway, perfect for those seeking tranquility and natural beauty.

5. Atherton Tablelands:

Escape the coastal heat and venture to the cooler climate of the Atherton Tablelands. This picturesque highland region is dotted with waterfalls, crater lakes, and fertile farmland.

Explore the mesmerizing Curtain Fig Tree, a unique natural attraction where the roots of a strangler fig cascade down like a curtain. Discover the cascading Millaa Millaa Falls, swim in the refreshing waters of Lake Eacham, and visit the charming villages of Yungaburra and Malanda. The Atherton Tablelands is a paradise for food lovers, offering farm-fresh produce, coffee plantations, and dairy farms where you can sample delectable cheeses.

6. Fitzroy Island:

Escape the mainland and set sail to Fitzroy Island, a tropical paradise just a short ferry ride from Cairns. Immerse yourself in the crystal-clear waters, snorkel over colorful coral reefs, or kayak along the coastline. Hike through lush rainforest trails, explore the underwater observatory, or simply relax on the white sandy beaches. Fitzroy Island offers a serene retreat for those seeking a tranquil island experience.

7. Tjapukai Aboriginal Cultural Park:

Discover the rich cultural heritage of the indigenous people of Australia at the Tjapukai Aboriginal Cultural Park. Engage in interactive performances, traditional dances, and storytelling sessions that provide a deep insight into the history, customs, and spirituality of the Aboriginal people. Participate in didgeridoo workshops, try your hand at spear throwing, and savor traditional bush tucker cuisine. The Tjapukai Cultural Park is a captivating place to gain a greater understanding of Australia's First Nations peoples.

Cairns and Tropical North Queensland offer an abundance of natural wonders and cultural treasures that make it a top destination for travelers. From the awe-inspiring Great Barrier Reef to the ancient Daintree Rainforest, this region provides an unforgettable experience for nature enthusiasts, adventure seekers, and those seeking a deeper connection with Australia's indigenous heritage. Whether you're exploring the underwater paradise, embarking on rainforest adventures, or immersing yourself in Aboriginal culture, Cairns and Tropical North Queensland promise an extraordinary journey that will leave you with lasting memories.

Daintree Rainforest

Nestled in the pristine region of Tropical North Queensland, the Daintree Rainforest stands as a magnificent natural wonder and one of Australia's most captivating attractions. With its lush greenery, diverse wildlife, and rich cultural heritage, the Daintree Rainforest offers a mesmerizing experience for nature enthusiasts and adventure seekers alike. As part of a comprehensive Australia travel guide, this article delves into the awe-inspiring beauty and unique features of the Daintree Rainforest, positioning it as a must-visit destination for travelers visiting Cairns and Tropical North Queensland.

1. A Natural Treasure Trove :

The Daintree Rainforest is a UNESCO World Heritage-listed site, renowned for its unparalleled biodiversity and ancient origins. Spanning over 1,200 square kilometers, it is the largest continuous area of tropical rainforest in Australia. This pristine ecosystem is home to an extraordinary array of plant and animal species, including rare and endemic ones found nowhere else on Earth. Towering fan palms, sprawling ferns, and ancient trees create a dense canopy that filters sunlight, creating an enchanting and serene environment for exploration.

2. Flora and Fauna :

The Daintree Rainforest boasts an astonishing diversity of flora and fauna. Visitors can encounter an extraordinary range of plant species, from towering strangler figs to vibrant orchids and delicate ferns. The region is also a sanctuary for numerous animal species, including the endangered southern cassowary, tree kangaroos, and the elusive Bennett's tree-kangaroo. Birdwatchers can rejoice as the rainforest is home to over 430 species of birds, including the iconic Australian riflebird and the vibrant kingfisher.

3. Indigenous Culture and Heritage :

The Daintree Rainforest holds deep cultural significance for the Indigenous Kuku Yalanji people, who have inhabited the region for thousands of years. Travelers have the opportunity to engage with the local Aboriginal communities and learn about their ancient traditions, spiritual connections to the land, and sustainable practices. Guided tours led by Indigenous elders provide valuable insights into the rainforest's cultural heritage, medicinal plants, and traditional hunting techniques.

4. Explore the Daintree :

Visitors to the Daintree Rainforest can embark on a multitude of thrilling adventures and immersive experiences. The region offers a variety of walking trails, allowing hikers to explore the diverse ecosystems and witness breathtaking vistas. The renowned Mossman Gorge presents an opportunity for a refreshing swim in crystal-clear waters surrounded by majestic boulders and dense rainforest.

A must-do activity is a cruise along the Daintree River, where knowledgeable guides offer fascinating insights into the ecosystem while spotting crocodiles, snakes, and other wildlife. For the more adventurous, zip-lining through the rainforest canopy provides a unique perspective, allowing you to soar above the treetops and witness the magnificent landscape from a thrilling vantage point.

5. Cape Tribulation :

Located within the Daintree Rainforest, Cape Tribulation is a place of exceptional beauty, where two UNESCO World Heritage sites converge: the rainforest and the Great Barrier Reef. This picturesque coastal region offers a stunning contrast of pristine beaches, lush rainforest, and sparkling turquoise waters. Visitors can explore the shoreline on horseback, take a guided sea kayaking tour, or venture into the depths of the Great Barrier Reef for an unforgettable snorkeling or diving experience.

6. Conservation and Sustainability :

Preserving the fragile ecosystem of the Daintree Rainforest is of utmost importance. Various organizations and initiatives work tirelessly to protect and conserve this unique environment. Visitors are encouraged to support sustainable tourism practices, such as eco-lodges, responsible guided tours, and respecting the natural habitat and wildlife.

As a top attraction of Cairns and Tropical North Queensland, the Daintree Rainforest offers an unrivaled opportunity to connect with nature, discover ancient traditions, and immerse oneself in the splendor of a pristine tropical rainforest. From its breathtaking flora and fauna to its captivating Indigenous heritage, the Daintree Rainforest provides an enriching and unforgettable experience for travelers seeking to explore Australia's natural wonders. By promoting sustainable tourism practices and embracing the ecological significance of this precious ecosystem, visitors can help ensure the preservation of the

Daintree Rainforest for generations to come. Plan your trip to Cairns and Tropical North Queensland, and let the magical allure of the Daintree Rainforest leave an indelible mark on your travel memories.

Kuranda Village

Cairns and Tropical North Queensland in Australia boast a wealth of natural wonders and cultural delights. Amidst this stunning region lies Kuranda Village, a top attraction that enthralls visitors with its unique charm. Nestled within the lush rainforest, Kuranda Village offers an immersive experience that combines breathtaking natural beauty with vibrant art, heritage, and wildlife encounters. This comprehensive Australia travel guide explores the allure of Kuranda Village, highlighting its captivating features, key attractions, and practical tips for an unforgettable visit.

1. Historical and Cultural Significance
Kuranda Village holds a rich history that dates back thousands of years, originally inhabited by the Djabugay Aboriginal people. European

settlement began in the late 1800s during the construction of the railway, which is still operational today. The village's heritage is evident through its well-preserved buildings, quaint markets, and vibrant arts scene.

2. Spectacular Natural Surroundings

One of the main draws of Kuranda Village is its remarkable natural surroundings. Situated in the heart of the World Heritage-listed Wet Tropics rainforest, the village is enveloped in a verdant oasis. Towering trees, cascading waterfalls, and winding trails create a captivating backdrop for exploration and relaxation. Visitors can embark on hikes through the rainforest, discovering its diverse flora and fauna, or take a scenic ride on the Skyrail Rainforest Cableway or the Kuranda Scenic Railway.

3. Vibrant Arts and Crafts

Kuranda Village has long been a hub for artists, artisans, and craftspeople. The village is home to numerous galleries, boutiques, and studios, where visitors can admire and purchase unique handcrafted treasures. The Kuranda Original Rainforest Markets are a highlight, offering a bustling marketplace where local artisans display their creations. From indigenous artwork and pottery to jewelry and clothing, the markets provide an authentic shopping experience.

4. Wildlife Encounters
For animal enthusiasts, Kuranda Village offers a range of exciting wildlife experiences. The Australian Butterfly Sanctuary, the largest butterfly exhibit in the Southern Hemisphere, delights visitors with its vibrant array of butterflies. The Kuranda Koala Gardens allow visitors to get up close and personal with Australia's most beloved marsupials, while the Birdworld Kuranda showcases a vast collection of exotic bird species. Additionally, the Rainforestation Nature Park provides opportunities to encounter native wildlife, including kangaroos, wallabies, and the elusive cassowary.

5. Cultural Experiences
To delve deeper into the cultural heritage of the region, visitors can participate in indigenous cultural tours and experiences. The Tjapukai Aboriginal Cultural Park offers interactive performances, guided walks, and storytelling sessions that provide insights into the traditions and customs of the local Djabugay people. Visitors can learn about traditional art,

music, and dance, gaining a deeper appreciation for Australia's indigenous heritage.

6. Practical Information and Tips

To make the most of a visit to Kuranda Village, it's advisable to plan ahead. The village is easily accessible from Cairns by either the Skyrail Rainforest Cableway or the Kuranda Scenic Railway. Both options offer breathtaking views and unique perspectives of the surrounding rainforest. It's recommended to allocate a full day to explore the village, ensuring ample time to discover its various attractions and experiences. Additionally, Kuranda Village provides a range of dining options, from casual cafes to fine dining restaurants, serving both local and international cuisine.

Kuranda Village stands out as a top attraction in Cairns and Tropical North Queensland, captivating visitors with its harmonious blend of natural beauty, cultural experiences, and wildlife encounters. Its historical significance, lush rainforest surroundings, vibrant arts scene, and unique wildlife encounters make it a must-visit destination for travelers seeking an authentic and immersive Australian experience. Whether strolling through the rainforest, admiring local artwork, or encountering native animals up close, Kuranda Village offers an enchanting escape that leaves a lasting impression on all who visit. So, add Kuranda Village to your itinerary and embark on a remarkable journey into the heart of Australia's tropical paradise.

Port Douglas

Port Douglas, a charming coastal town located in Tropical North Queensland, Australia, is a true gem and a top attraction for visitors exploring the Cairns region. Situated just an hour's drive north of Cairns, this idyllic destination offers a unique blend of natural beauty, adventure, and relaxation. With its pristine beaches, lush rainforests, and proximity to the Great Barrier Reef, Port Douglas is a paradise for nature lovers and adventure enthusiasts. In this comprehensive Australia travel guide, we will delve into the many attractions and activities that make Port Douglas a must-visit destination, exploring its stunning landscapes, vibrant marine life, luxury resorts, and cultural experiences.

1. Natural Wonders

Port Douglas boasts an array of natural wonders that showcase the region's diverse and breathtaking landscapes. Four Mile Beach, a palm-fringed stretch of white sand, is a popular spot for swimming, sunbathing, and beach strolls. It provides a picturesque backdrop to the town and offers stunning views of the Coral Sea. The nearby Flagstaff Hill lookout offers panoramic vistas of the coastline and the surrounding rainforest-clad mountains.

One of the main highlights of Port Douglas is its proximity to the world-renowned Great Barrier Reef, a UNESCO World Heritage site. Visitors can embark on snorkeling or diving excursions to explore this vibrant underwater ecosystem teeming with colorful coral formations and diverse marine life. The Low Isles, a small coral cay located just a short boat ride away, is a popular destination for day trips, offering pristine snorkeling opportunities and guided nature walks.

For those seeking an encounter with the ancient rainforests of Tropical North Queensland, a visit to the Daintree Rainforest is a must. This UNESCO-listed rainforest is one of the oldest in the world, home to a remarkable diversity of plant and animal species. Guided tours allow visitors to explore this lush wilderness, discover rare wildlife such as the endangered Southern Cassowary, and learn about the indigenous culture and traditions of the local Kuku Yalanji people.

2. Adventure and Outdoor Activities

Port Douglas is a playground for outdoor enthusiasts, offering a wide range of thrilling activities and adventures. The nearby Mossman Gorge provides opportunities for swimming in crystal-clear waters, hiking through the rainforest, and experiencing the beauty of cascading waterfalls. The rugged terrain of the nearby Daintree National Park is perfect for adventurous souls who wish to go hiking, zip-lining, or embark on 4WD tours to explore its hidden gems.

Another popular activity in Port Douglas is fishing, with the region being known for its rich marine biodiversity. Visitors can join fishing charters to try their luck at catching barramundi, coral trout, and other prized species. The rivers and estuaries surrounding Port Douglas also offer excellent opportunities for kayaking and stand-up paddleboarding, allowing visitors to immerse themselves in the serene beauty of the coastal waterways.

Thrill-seekers can take to the skies with scenic helicopter rides or hot air balloon tours, offering breathtaking views of the Great Barrier Reef, Daintree Rainforest, and the stunning coastline. The nearby Atherton Tablelands, with its waterfalls, crater lakes, and rolling green hills, is another popular destination for adventure activities such as mountain biking, horseback riding, and quad biking.

3. Luxury Resorts and Relaxation

Port Douglas is renowned for its luxury resorts and world-class accommodation options that cater to travelers seeking relaxation and indulgence. From boutique hotels to exclusive beachfront resorts, there are accommodations to suit every taste and budget. Many resorts offer private access to Four Mile Beach, ensuring guests can enjoy the pristine shoreline at their leisure.

The town's main street, Macrossan Street, is lined with boutique shops, galleries, and a plethora of dining options ranging from casual cafes to award-winning restaurants. Visitors can savor the fresh flavors of local seafood, tropical fruits, and regional specialties, accompanied by fine wines from nearby vineyards.

Spas and wellness centers in Port Douglas provide the perfect opportunity to unwind and rejuvenate. Offering a range of therapeutic treatments inspired by indigenous traditions and utilizing natural ingredients, these wellness retreats are designed to promote relaxation and well-being.

4. Cultural Experiences

Port Douglas offers visitors a chance to immerse themselves in the rich cultural heritage of the region. The Port Douglas Sunday Market is a popular attraction, showcasing local artisans, fresh produce, and live music. Visitors can browse through a variety of handmade crafts, jewelry, and locally sourced products.

The region is also home to several art galleries that exhibit the works of local and indigenous artists, providing insight into the unique artistic traditions of the area. The Flames of the Forest, an immersive cultural experience, offers visitors the opportunity to dine under the stars while enjoying live music and storytelling by the fireside, providing a deeper understanding of the traditions and history of the indigenous people.

For those interested in indigenous culture, guided tours led by local Aboriginal guides provide an educational and enlightening experience. Visitors can learn about the traditional uses of plants and discover the spiritual significance of the land through storytelling and traditional ceremonies.

Port Douglas, with its natural beauty, adventure opportunities, luxury resorts, and cultural experiences, is undeniably a top attraction of Cairns and Tropical North Queensland. Whether you're seeking relaxation on pristine beaches, thrilling adventures in the Great Barrier Reef and rainforests, or a luxurious getaway in a world-class resort, Port Douglas offers something for everyone. Its accessibility to iconic natural wonders, coupled with its vibrant cultural scene, makes it an ideal destination for travelers looking to explore the best of Australia's tropical paradise. So pack your bags, immerse yourself in the wonders of Port Douglas, and create unforgettable memories in this slice of paradise.

• Outdoor Activities and Adventure

Cairns and Tropical North Queensland in Australia are renowned for their natural beauty, vibrant ecosystems, and thrilling outdoor adventures. With a stunning combination of lush rainforests, pristine beaches, and the iconic Great Barrier Reef, this region offers an array of exciting activities for adventure enthusiasts and nature lovers alike. In this Australia travel guide, we will explore the top outdoor activities and adventures in Cairns and Tropical North Queensland.

1. Snorkeling and Diving at the Great Barrier Reef:

One of the most extraordinary experiences in this region is exploring the Great Barrier Reef, the world's largest coral reef system. Visitors can embark on snorkeling or diving excursions to witness the breathtaking underwater world teeming with vibrant coral formations, tropical fish, and other marine life. Several tour operators offer day trips and liveaboard experiences, providing opportunities for both beginners and experienced divers to discover the wonders of this UNESCO World Heritage Site.

2. Rainforest Exploration:

Cairns and its surrounding areas are blessed with ancient rainforests, offering a chance to immerse yourself in the incredible biodiversity of the region. The Daintree Rainforest, a UNESCO World Heritage-listed site, is a must-visit destination. Explore its lush trails, take a river cruise to spot crocodiles, or venture into the canopy on a thrilling zipline tour. Another notable rainforest destination is the Atherton Tablelands, where you can discover stunning waterfalls, volcanic lakes, and diverse wildlife.

3. Whitewater Rafting:

For those seeking adrenaline-pumping adventures, whitewater rafting is an excellent choice. The Tully River, located south of Cairns, provides thrilling rapids and challenging sections for rafting enthusiasts. Join a guided tour and navigate through the river's twists and turns, experiencing the rush of the cascading waters amidst the tropical rainforest backdrop. With different levels of difficulty available, this activity caters to both beginners and experienced rafters.

4. Skydiving:

For an exhilarating experience and a bird's-eye view of the region's spectacular landscapes, skydiving is an absolute must. Take a leap from an aircraft and freefall through the sky before enjoying a scenic parachute ride back to the ground. Imagine the rush of adrenaline as you soar over the Great Barrier Reef, lush rainforests, and golden beaches. With professional instructors and breathtaking views, skydiving in Cairns guarantees an unforgettable adventure.

5. Bungee Jumping:

If you're a thrill-seeker looking for the ultimate adrenaline rush, consider bungee jumping. Located just 20 minutes from Cairns, the AJ Hackett Bungy site offers a 50-meter leap of faith into a lush rainforest setting. Experience the heart-pounding sensation as you dive headfirst towards the ground, only to be recoiled by the elastic cord, leaving you with an incredible feeling of accomplishment.

6. Hot Air Ballooning:

Witness the stunning sunrise over the Atherton Tablelands as you embark on a hot air balloon ride. Drift gently above the rolling hills, lush farmland, and ancient rainforests while taking in panoramic views of the surrounding landscape. This serene and enchanting experience provides a unique perspective on Tropical North Queensland's natural beauty and is perfect for those seeking a more relaxed adventure.

7. Wildlife Encounters:

Tropical North Queensland is home to a diverse range of wildlife, and visitors have ample opportunities to engage with these fascinating creatures. Explore the Wildlife Habitat in Port Douglas to get up close and personal with kangaroos, koalas, and crocodiles. For a truly unique experience, head to Hartley's Crocodile Adventures, where you can observe crocodiles in their natural habitat and even participate in a thrilling boat cruise.

8. Island Hopping and Beach Activities:

The Cairns region is blessed with numerous stunning islands, each offering its unique charm. Take a day trip to Fitzroy Island or Green Island, where you can relax on pristine beaches, snorkel amidst coral gardens, or take a glass-bottom boat tour. For a more secluded experience, consider visiting the idyllic Low Isles, offering a tranquil escape with its white sandy beaches and colorful marine life.

Cairns and Tropical North Queensland in Australia provide an abundance of outdoor activities and adventures for travelers seeking an adrenaline rush or a deep connection with nature. From exploring the mesmerizing Great Barrier Reef to venturing into ancient rainforests, this region offers a diverse range of experiences. Whether you're snorkeling in crystal-clear waters, freefalling from the sky, or encountering unique wildlife, Cairns and Tropical North Queensland are sure to leave you with unforgettable memories of your Australian adventure.

• *Indigenous Culture and Heritage*

Cairns and Tropical North Queensland in Australia are renowned for their stunning natural landscapes, diverse wildlife, and vibrant cultural experiences. Central to the region's rich tapestry is its Indigenous culture and heritage, which dates back thousands of years. This travel guide aims to delve into the unique and captivating world of Indigenous Australia, providing insights into the traditions, art, history, and spiritual connections of the local Aboriginal and Torres

Strait Islander communities. From ancient rock art to immersive cultural experiences, discover the essence of Indigenous culture in Cairns and Tropical North Queensland.

1. A Brief Overview of Indigenous History:

To truly appreciate the Indigenous culture of Cairns and Tropical North Queensland, it is essential to understand the historical context. Indigenous Australians have inhabited this region for over 40,000 years, cultivating deep connections with the land, sea, and sky. The region is home to several Aboriginal and Torres Strait Islander groups, each with their own distinct language, traditions, and customs.

2. Indigenous Art and Craft:

Indigenous art is a powerful medium that encapsulates the stories, spirituality, and connection to the land. Visitors to Cairns and Tropical North Queensland have the opportunity to witness and engage with various forms of Indigenous art. The Cairns Regional Gallery and the Tjapukai Aboriginal Cultural Park are excellent places to discover contemporary and traditional artworks, including paintings, sculptures, textiles, and intricately crafted artifacts. Additionally, visitors can explore local markets and art galleries to purchase authentic Indigenous artworks and support local artists.

3. Traditional Cultural Experiences:

Immersing oneself in traditional Indigenous cultural experiences is an invaluable way to gain a deeper understanding of the region's heritage. The Tjapukai Aboriginal Cultural Park offers interactive activities, dance performances, and storytelling sessions that provide insight into the customs, rituals, and Dreamtime legends of the local Djabugay people. Visitors can participate in boomerang throwing, spear-throwing, and traditional dance workshops, fostering a sense of connection and appreciation for Indigenous traditions.

4. Indigenous Guided Tours and Walks:

Embarking on an Indigenous-guided tour or walk enables visitors to explore the breathtaking landscapes of Cairns and Tropical North Queensland while learning about the region's ancient Indigenous heritage. Journey with knowledgeable guides to discover hidden rock art sites, sacred ceremonial grounds, and significant cultural landmarks. The Mossman Gorge Centre offers guided walks led by the local Kuku Yalanji people, providing insights into their traditions, medicinal plant knowledge, and spiritual beliefs.

5. Cultural Festivals and Events:
Throughout the year, Cairns and Tropical North Queensland come alive with vibrant cultural festivals and events that showcase the diversity and richness of Indigenous heritage. The Cairns Indigenous Art Fair (CIAF) is a highlight, featuring exhibitions, dance performances, workshops, and traditional ceremonies. The Yarrabah Band Festival and Laura Aboriginal Dance Festival are other notable events where visitors can witness captivating performances, music, and dance.

6. Exploring Ancient Rock Art:
The region is home to some of the most significant rock art sites in Australia, offering a glimpse into the ancient traditions and stories of the Indigenous people. The Quinkan Galleries, located near Laura, house rock art dating back thousands of years, depicting ancestral beings, animals, and cultural practices. With the guidance of local Indigenous rangers, visitors can experience the awe-inspiring beauty of these sacred sites and

gain a deeper understanding of their cultural significance.

7. Aboriginal and Torres Strait Islander Cultural Centers:

Cairns and Tropical North Queensland are home to several Aboriginal and Torres Strait Islander cultural centers that provide valuable insights into the diverse Indigenous cultures of the region. The Djumbunji Press in Mossman offers an opportunity
to witness the traditional process of printmaking, while the Gab Titui Cultural Centre on Thursday Island showcases Torres Strait Islander art, history, and traditional practices. These centers serve as important hubs for preserving, promoting, and sharing Indigenous knowledge and traditions.

Cairns and Tropical North Queensland offer a wealth of experiences to immerse oneself in the rich Indigenous culture and heritage of Australia. From engaging with contemporary artworks to witnessing ancient rock art, participating in traditional cultural activities, and attending vibrant festivals, visitors can gain a profound appreciation for the depth and diversity of Indigenous traditions. By supporting local Indigenous artists and engaging in cultural exchanges, travelers can contribute to the preservation and celebration of Australia's Indigenous culture for future generations to come.

•Dining and Shopping

Cairns and Tropical North Queensland are renowned for their stunning natural landscapes, including the Great Barrier Reef and the Daintree Rainforest. However, the region also offers a delightful array of dining and shopping experiences that are sure to satisfy even the most discerning travelers. In this guide, we will explore the vibrant culinary scene and unique shopping opportunities in Cairns and Tropical North Queensland.

I. Dining Experiences:

1. Seafood Delights:

- Being located near the coast, Cairns and Tropical North Queensland are a paradise for seafood lovers. Fresh catches of the day, including succulent prawns, crabs, barramundi, and coral trout, can be found at local seafood markets and restaurants.

- The Pier at the Marlin Marina in Cairns is a popular dining spot with a wide range of seafood options, offering picturesque waterfront views and a relaxed ambiance.

2. Indigenous Cuisine:

   - Experience the rich flavors of traditional Indigenous Australian cuisine. Many restaurants in the region offer a unique fusion of Indigenous ingredients and contemporary cooking techniques, such as kangaroo, bush tomatoes, and lemon myrtle.

   - Try Tjapukai Aboriginal Cultural Park's Flame Tree Bar & Grill for an authentic Indigenous dining experience featuring dishes inspired by ancient traditions.

3. Tropical Delicacies:

   - Indulge in the tropical delights of the region, including exotic fruits like mangoes, papayas, and bananas. Tropical flavors can be found in a variety of dishes and desserts across the region's restaurants and cafes.

   - Rusty's Market in Cairns is a bustling marketplace where you can find an abundance of fresh tropical fruits, along with other local produce and international delicacies.

4. International Cuisine:

   - Cairns and Tropical North Queensland cater to a diverse range of tastes with their international culinary offerings. From Italian and Asian to Mediterranean and Middle

Eastern cuisine, there is something for everyone.

- The vibrant restaurant scene in Cairns' Esplanade offers a multitude of dining options, ensuring that visitors can savor flavors from around the world.

II. Shopping Experiences:
1. Cairns Central Shopping Centre:

   - Located in the heart of Cairns, this modern shopping center is home to a variety of fashion, beauty, and lifestyle stores. With over 180 specialty stores, it offers an excellent retail therapy experience.

2. Rusty's Market:

   - As mentioned earlier, Rusty's Market is not only a haven for fresh produce but also a fantastic shopping destination. Wander through the vibrant stalls to discover unique crafts, clothing, accessories, and souvenirs.

3. Kuranda Markets:

   - A visit to Kuranda, a picturesque village nestled in the rainforest, is incomplete without exploring its famous markets. The markets are filled with local artisans showcasing their handmade jewelry, artwork, clothing, and indigenous crafts.

4. Port Douglas Sunday Markets:

   - Just an hour's drive from Cairns, Port Douglas hosts lively Sunday markets. Here, you can find an array of local products, including handmade crafts, jewelry, fashion, and fresh produce.

5. Aboriginal Art:

   - Cairns and Tropical North Queensland are known for their thriving Aboriginal art scene. Visit art galleries and cultural centers to admire and purchase unique indigenous artworks, including paintings, sculptures, and textiles.

Cairns and Tropical North Queensland offer a remarkable fusion of culinary delights and shopping experiences. From indulging in fresh seafood and tropical delicacies to exploring local markets and immersing in the region's indigenous culture, there is no shortage of options to satisfy your appetite and fulfill your shopping desires. With its vibrant dining scene and diverse shopping opportunities, this region of Australia promises an unforgettable journey of flavors and treasures for every traveler.

CHAPTER SEVEN

Perth and Western Australia

•*Overview of Perth and Western Australia*

Located on the pristine western coastline of Australia, Perth and Western Australia are captivating destinations that offer an array of unique experiences for travelers. With its stunning landscapes, vibrant cities, and diverse wildlife, this region holds something special for every type of adventurer. In this comprehensive travel guide, we will delve into the remarkable attractions, cultural highlights, outdoor adventures, and culinary delights that make Perth and Western Australia a must-visit destination for all.

I. Geography and Climate:

1. Geographical Features:

a. Vast Outback: Western Australia boasts expansive desert regions such as the Great Victoria Desert and the Gibson Desert, offering a true Australian outback experience.

b. Coastal Beauty: The state is blessed with over 12,000 kilometers of pristine coastline, including the world-famous Ningaloo Reef and the rugged cliffs of the Margaret River region.

2. Climate:

a. Mediterranean Climate: Perth enjoys a Mediterranean climate with hot, dry summers and mild, wet winters, making it an ideal year-round destination.

b. Tropical Climate: As you travel north, the climate becomes more tropical, with warmer temperatures and higher humidity in regions like Broome and the Kimberley.

II. Perth - The Capital City:

1. City Highlights:

a. Kings Park and Botanic Garden: A sprawling urban park offering stunning city views, native flora, and a tranquil environment.

b. Fremantle: A charming port city known for its maritime history, vibrant markets, and alfresco dining along the waterfront.

c. Swan River: Explore the river on a scenic cruise or enjoy watersports such as kayaking and paddleboarding.

d. Perth Cultural Centre: Home to art galleries, museums, and the State Library of

Western Australia, showcasing the region's rich history and contemporary art scene.

e. Perth Beaches: Relax on the golden sands of Cottesloe Beach, Scarborough Beach, or the secluded beaches of Rottnest Island.

2. Rottnest Island:

a. Encounter Quokkas: Rottnest Island is famous for its adorable resident marsupials, the quokkas. Take a selfie with these friendly creatures.

b. Stunning Beaches: Explore the island's 63 beaches, snorkel in crystal-clear waters, or go on a thrilling diving adventure to discover shipwrecks.

III. Margaret River Wine Region:

1. Wine and Gastronomy:

a. Wineries and Cellar Doors: Discover world-class wineries, cellar doors, and vineyard restaurants offering exquisite wine-tasting experiences.

b. Gourmet Delights: Indulge in locally produced cheeses, chocolates, and fresh seafood, complemented by premium wines.

2. Natural Wonders:

a. Caves and Karri Forests: Explore the majestic caves and towering karri forests, such as Jewel Cave and Boranup Forest.

b. Surfing and Beaches: Margaret River is renowned for its world-class surf breaks, attracting surfers from around the globe.

IV. Exquisite Coastal Escapes:

1. Ningaloo Reef:

a. Snorkeling and Diving: Immerse yourself in the vibrant underwater world of Ningaloo Reef, swimming alongside whale sharks, manta rays, and turtles.

b. Cape Range National Park: Experience the rugged beauty of the national park, with stunning gorges, canyons, and secluded beaches.

2. Broome:

a. Cable Beach: Enjoy breathtaking sunsets and camel rides along the 22-kilometer-long Cable Beach, known for its white sand and turquoise waters.

b. Staircase to the Moon: Witness the natural phenomenon of the

Staircase to the Moon, where the full moon reflects on the tidal flats.

V. Outdoor Adventures:

1. Kimberley Region:

a. Bungle Bungle Range: Discover the remarkable beehive-shaped formations of the Bungle Bungle Range in Purnululu National Park.

b. Horizontal Falls: Experience the exhilarating tidal phenomenon of the Horizontal Falls, accessible via scenic flights or boat tours.

2. Wave Rock:

a. Awe-Inspiring Rock Formation: Visit Wave Rock, a natural rock formation resembling an enormous ocean wave, located near the town of Hyden.

Perth and Western Australia offer an unparalleled blend of natural wonders, cosmopolitan cities, and unique cultural experiences. From the bustling streets of Perth to the stunning coastline, wine regions, and captivating outback landscapes, this region promises an unforgettable adventure for travelers seeking to explore the beauty and diversity of Australia. Embrace the charm of Perth and venture out into Western Australia to discover its hidden treasures, enriching your travel experience with a tapestry of unforgettable memories.

• *Top Attractions*

Perth, the capital city of Western Australia, is a captivating destination that boasts a perfect blend of natural beauty, cultural vibrancy, and a laid-back lifestyle. Western Australia, on the other hand, is a vast and diverse region that offers a plethora of attractions to explore. From pristine beaches and breathtaking landscapes to vibrant cities and unique wildlife encounters, there is something for everyone in this part of Australia. In this comprehensive travel guide, we will delve into the top attractions of Perth and Western Australia, giving you an insight into the must-visit places and experiences that will make your trip truly unforgettable.

1. *Kings Park and Botanic Garden:*

Located in the heart of Perth, Kings Park and Botanic Garden is one of the largest inner-city parks in the world, offering stunning views of the city skyline and the Swan River. This sprawling parkland features an extensive collection of native plants, serene walking trails, beautiful picnic spots, and the iconic Lotterywest Federation Walkway, a glass bridge that takes you through the treetops.

2. Rottnest Island:

Just a short ferry ride away from Perth, Rottnest Island is a true gem of Western Australia. Known for its pristine beaches, crystal-clear waters, and unique wildlife, the island is home to the adorable quokkas, a friendly marsupial found only in this region. Explore the island on a bike, snorkel in the vibrant coral reefs, and relax on the stunning beaches, such as The Basin and Pinky Beach.

3. Pinnacles Desert:

Located within Nambung National Park, the Pinnacles Desert is a surreal and otherworldly landscape of limestone formations. These towering pillars rise from the golden sands, creating a mesmerizing sight. Explore the desert on foot or take a scenic drive to witness the magical play of light and shadows during sunrise or sunset.

4. Margaret River:

Situated in the southwest region of Western Australia, Margaret River is a paradise for food and wine enthusiasts. This picturesque area is renowned for its world-class wineries, gourmet restaurants, and breathtaking coastal scenery. Indulge in wine tastings, sample delicious local produce, and soak in the beauty of beaches like Prevelly and Meelup.

5. Ningaloo Reef:

For an unforgettable marine adventure, head to Ningaloo Reef, located in the Coral Coast region of Western Australia. This World Heritage-listed site is home to an abundance of marine life, including whale sharks, manta rays, turtles, and vibrant coral formations. Snorkel or dive to explore the pristine underwater world, or join a whale shark tour for an up-close encounter with these gentle giants.

6. Wave Rock:

Situated in the Wheatbelt region, Wave Rock is a natural rock formation that resembles a massive ocean wave frozen in time. This unique geological wonder attracts visitors from around the world, who come to marvel at its impressive size and colorful banding. Take a walk around the base of the rock and learn about its Aboriginal significance and the surrounding wildlife.

7. Perth Cultural Centre:

Immerse yourself in the vibrant arts and cultural scene of Perth at the Perth Cultural Centre. This precinct houses several cultural institutions, including the Art Gallery of Western Australia, the Western Australian Museum, the State Library of Western Australia, and the Perth Institute of Contemporary Arts. Explore the galleries, attend live performances, and discover the rich history and heritage of the region.

8. Monkey Mia:

Located in the Shark Bay World Heritage Area, Monkey Mia is a must-visit destination for animal lovers. This famous beach is known for its daily dolphin feeding experience, where wild bottlenose dolphins come close to shore to interact with visitors. Witness these intelligent creatures up close and learn about their conservation efforts in the area.

9. The Kimberley:

For those seeking rugged beauty and adventure, the Kimberley region in the northern part of Western Australia is a dream come true. This vast and remote wilderness is characterized by dramatic gorges, cascading waterfalls, ancient rock formations, and expansive outback landscapes. Explore the Bungle Bungle Range in Purnululu National Park, take a cruise along the stunning Geikie Gorge, or hike through the majestic Mitchell Falls.

10. Cape Le Grand National Park:

Located near the town of Esperance, Cape Le Grand National Park showcases some of Australia's most stunning beaches. With its pristine white sands, crystal-clear turquoise waters, and granite peaks, the park offers breathtaking scenery and a range of outdoor activities. Don't miss the chance to climb Frenchman Peak for panoramic views or swim at the iconic Lucky Bay, known for its resident kangaroos.

Perth and Western Australia present a diverse range of attractions that cater to nature enthusiasts, adventure seekers, beach lovers, and culture aficionados alike. From the urban charm of Perth to the rugged wilderness of the Kimberley, this region is a treasure trove of unforgettable experiences. Whether you are exploring the unique flora and fauna, indulging in world-class food and wine, or simply basking in the natural beauty, Perth and Western Australia will undoubtedly leave a lasting impression on every traveler fortunate enough to visit.

Kings Park and Botanic Garden

Australia is a land of breathtaking natural wonders, and among its many treasures lies Kings Park and Botanic Garden. Located in the heart of Perth, Western Australia, this expansive parkland offers visitors an immersive experience with stunning landscapes, diverse flora and fauna, and rich cultural heritage. Spanning over 400 hectares,

Kings Park is one of the largest inner-city parks in the world and holds a special place in the hearts of locals and tourists alike. This travel guide will take you on a journey through the beauty and charm of Kings Park and Botanic Garden, offering insights into its history, attractions, and activities.

History and Significance

Kings Park and Botanic Garden holds great historical and cultural significance. Originally established in 1872 as the Perth Park, it was renamed Kings Park in 1901 to commemorate the coronation of King Edward VII. Over the years, the park has evolved into a thriving botanical garden, showcasing Western Australia's unique plant species and preserving its natural heritage. The parkland also has deep cultural significance to the Whadjuk Noongar people, the traditional owners of the land, who have a strong spiritual connection to this place.

Attractions and Gardens

Kings Park and Botanic Garden offers a myriad of attractions that cater to every visitor's interests. The park is home to an extensive collection of native plants, including over 3,000 species of Western Australian flora. The Western Australian Botanic Garden within

Kings Park is a particular highlight, featuring meticulously curated gardens that showcase different ecosystems and plant communities. Some notable gardens include the Banksias Garden, Eucalyptus Garden, and the Acacia Garden, each offering a unique display of native flora.

One of the most iconic features of Kings Park is the Lotterywest Federation Walkway, a treetop walk that offers panoramic views of the Swan River, Perth skyline, and the surrounding parklands. Visitors can also explore the DNA Tower, an impressive 15-story high spiral structure that provides breathtaking views from its top.

The Synergy Parkland is a popular family-friendly area within Kings Park, featuring a playground, picnic facilities, and vast open spaces for leisurely activities. It is also home to the Rio Tinto Naturescape, an immersive nature play space designed to reconnect children with the natural world.

Cultural Heritage and Memorials

Kings Park and Botanic Garden is not only a haven for nature enthusiasts but also a site of cultural significance and remembrance. The

State War Memorial Precinct stands as a solemn tribute to the brave servicemen and women who sacrificed their lives in various conflicts. The majestic Cenotaph, Flame of Remembrance, and the Court of Contemplation form the centerpiece of this precinct, providing a tranquil space for reflection and commemoration.

Another notable memorial within Kings Park is the Kings Park War Memorial, which honors the fallen soldiers of World War I. The memorial features the iconic 'Winged Victory' sculpture, surrounded by serene gardens and water features. It is a poignant reminder of the sacrifices made by Australian troops.

Events and Festivals

Throughout the year, Kings Park and Botanic Garden hosts a range of events and festivals that celebrate nature, culture, and community. The Kings Park Festival, held annually in September, showcases the park's vibrant wildflower displays with guided walks, exhibitions, and live entertainment. The Perth International Arts Festival also features outdoor performances and installations within the park, adding a touch of artistic flair to the natural surroundings.

Recreational Activities

Kings Park offers a wealth of recreational activities for visitors to enjoy. The park has an extensive network of walking and cycling trails that meander through the lush greenery, providing an opportunity to immerse oneself in nature. Additionally, the Botanic Garden hosts regular guided walks and educational programs to enhance visitors' understanding of Western Australia's unique flora.

For those seeking adventure, the Lotterywest Family Area offers a 75-meter-long suspension bridge known as the Elevated Tree Walk. This thrilling experience allows visitors to walk among the treetops, offering a unique perspective of the park's diverse ecosystem.

Dining and Amenities

Kings Park and Botanic Garden boasts several dining options that cater to various tastes. The Botanical Café, nestled within the park, offers a delightful menu featuring locally sourced ingredients and stunning views of the gardens. Visitors can also enjoy a picnic in one of the designated areas while taking in the picturesque surroundings.

The park is well-equipped with amenities such as restrooms, visitor information centers, and souvenir shops, ensuring a comfortable and convenient experience for all.

Kings Park and Botanic Garden is an exquisite gem within the vibrant city of Perth, Western Australia. Its diverse gardens, rich cultural heritage, and breathtaking vistas make it a must-visit destination for nature lovers and history enthusiasts alike. Whether you're exploring the native flora, paying respects at the war memorials, or simply enjoying a leisurely stroll through the parklands, Kings Park offers an immersive and unforgettable experience. So, when planning your Australian adventure, be sure to include Kings Park and Botanic Garden in your itinerary for a truly memorable and enchanting experience.

Rottnest Island

Rottnest Island, located just 18 kilometers off the coast of Perth in Western Australia, is a hidden gem that offers a unique and unforgettable travel experience. Known for its stunning natural beauty, pristine beaches, and abundant wildlife, this island paradise attracts visitors from all over the world. With its rich history, diverse marine life, and relaxed atmosphere, Rottnest Island provides the perfect escape for nature lovers, beach enthusiasts, and adventure seekers. In this comprehensive Australia travel guide, we will delve into the captivating allure of Rottnest Island, providing insights into its history, attractions, activities, accommodation options, and practical tips for a memorable visit.

1. Historical Background

Rottnest Island has a fascinating history that dates back thousands of years. It was originally inhabited by the Noongar Aboriginal people, who called it "Wadjemup" and regarded it as a spiritual place. European exploration of the island began in the 17th century when Dutch navigator Willem de Vlamingh encountered a unique marsupial species, now known as the quokka, and named the island "Rotte Nest" (meaning "rat's nest" in Dutch) due to the abundance of these adorable creatures.

In the early 19th century, Rottnest Island served as a colonial prison, housing Aboriginal prisoners and later, convicts from the mainland. Many buildings from this period, such as the Rottnest Island Museum and the iconic Oliver Hill Battery, remain as reminders of the island's dark past. Today, Rottnest Island is recognized for its significant cultural heritage, and visitors can explore its historical sites and gain insights into its complex past.

2. Natural Beauty and Wildlife

Rottnest Island boasts a stunning natural landscape characterized by turquoise waters, white sandy beaches, and picturesque bays. With over 63 stunning beaches and 20 crystal-clear bays, visitors are spoiled for choice when it comes to soaking up the sun and enjoying water activities. Some of the must-visit beaches include The Basin, Little Parakeet Bay, and Pinky Beach, each offering its own unique charm and breathtaking views.

One of the island's most beloved inhabitants is the quokka, a small marsupial known for its friendly and photogenic nature. These adorable creatures can be found all over the island, and visitors have the opportunity to snap some memorable selfies with them. Rottnest Island is one of the few places in the world where you can encounter these friendly marsupials up close.

In addition to quokkas, Rottnest Island is home to an abundance of marine life, making it a haven for snorkeling and diving enthusiasts.

The waters surrounding the island are teeming with colorful coral reefs, tropical fish, and other fascinating sea creatures. Popular dive sites include Parker Point and Fish Hook Bay, where you can explore underwater caves, swim with dolphins, and spot majestic stingrays.

3. Attractions and Activities
Rottnest Island offers a myriad of attractions and activities to suit every interest and age group. Whether you're seeking adventure, relaxation, or cultural enrichment, this island paradise has something for everyone.

a. Exploration and Sightseeing:
Rent a bicycle or take a guided bus tour to explore the island's beauty at your own pace. Visit the Wadjemup Lighthouse, which offers panoramic views of the island, or take a stroll along the boardwalks at the West End to admire the rugged coastal scenery. The Oliver Hill Battery, a remnant of the island's military history, provides a glimpse into its past and offers breathtaking views from its vantage point.

b. Water Sports and

Recreation:

Indulge in an array of water activities, including swimming, snorkeling, kayaking, and paddleboarding. The pristine waters surrounding the island are perfect for exploring the vibrant marine life and coral reefs. Adventure seekers can try their hand at surfing or join a thrilling jet ski tour around the island.

c. Cultural Experiences:
Discover the island's rich cultural heritage by visiting the Rottnest Island Museum, which showcases the island's history, including its Aboriginal heritage. Explore the Indigenous Heritage Trail, where you can learn about the Noongar people's connection to the island and their traditional way of life.

d. Wildlife Encounters:
Embark on a wildlife tour or take a guided walking tour to spot various bird species, including the iconic ospreys and wedge-tailed eagles. Join a snorkeling tour to swim alongside playful dolphins and sea lions, or go whale watching during the migration season (September to November) to catch a glimpse of majestic humpback whales.

4. Accommodation and Dining Options

Rottnest Island offers a range of accommodation options to suit different budgets and preferences. From budget-friendly camping sites to luxurious beachfront villas, there is something for everyone. Popular choices include the Karma Rottnest, a historic hotel, and the Rottnest Lodge, offering modern amenities and breathtaking ocean views.

When it comes to dining, the island offers an eclectic mix of culinary delights. Enjoy fresh seafood at one of the waterfront restaurants, savor delicious pub fare at the Quokka Arms, or grab a quick bite from one of the island's cafes and bakeries. Don't forget to try the island's famous "Rottnest Bakery" for mouthwatering pies and pastries.

5. Practical Tips and Getting There
To make the most of your visit to Rottnest Island, here are some practical tips:

a. Getting There:
The island can be reached via a 25-minute ferry ride from Perth or Fremantle. Ferry services operate daily, and it's advisable to book your tickets in advance, especially during peak season. You can also opt for scenic helicopter

or seaplane flights for a truly memorable experience.

b. Getting Around:
Bicycles are the most popular mode of transport on the island, and they can be rented from several providers near the ferry terminals. Alternatively, a hop-on-hop-off bus service is available for those who prefer a guided tour.

c. Climate and Packing Essentials:
Rottnest Island enjoys a Mediterranean climate, with warm summers and mild winters. Pack sunscreen, a hat, and comfortable beachwear for the sunny days, and a light jacket for cooler evenings. Don't forget your snorkeling gear if you plan to explore the underwater world.

d. Booking Accommodation:
Due to its popularity, it's recommended to book your accommodation well in advance, especially during peak seasons and school holidays.

e. Respect for Wildlife and Environment:
While interacting with the quokkas, it's important to remember that they are wild animals. Maintain a safe distance and avoid

feeding them human food, as it can be harmful to their health. Additionally, respect the island's natural beauty by following the designated walking trails and taking all litter with you.

Rottnest Island is a slice of paradise that offers a diverse range of experiences, from exploring its rich history to immersing oneself in its natural beauty. With its stunning beaches, abundant wildlife, and a wide array of activities, it is no wonder that Rottnest Island is a must-visit destination for travelers to Western Australia. Whether you're seeking adventure, relaxation, or a deeper understanding of Australia's cultural heritage, this island sanctuary has it all. So, pack your bags, hop on a ferry, and prepare for an

Margaret River Region

The Margaret River Region, nestled in the southwestern corner of Western Australia, is a captivating destination that beckons travelers with its natural beauty, world-class wineries, pristine beaches, and an abundance of outdoor adventures. Located about 280 kilometers south of Perth, this enchanting region is a must-visit for anyone seeking an authentic Australian experience. With its stunning landscapes, diverse wildlife, and thriving arts and culinary scene, the Margaret River Region offers a wealth of attractions and activities to suit every traveler's preferences. In this comprehensive Australia travel guide, we will delve into the essence of this remarkable destination, exploring its captivating highlights, unearthing hidden gems, and providing invaluable tips to make the most of your visit.

1. Discovering the Natural Beauty

The Margaret River Region boasts an awe-inspiring natural beauty that captivates visitors from the moment they arrive. With its lush forests, rolling vineyards, and breathtaking coastline, this region is a nature lover's paradise. Start your adventure by exploring the towering karri trees of Boranup Forest or embarking on scenic hikes along the Cape to Cape Track, which offers stunning views of the rugged coastline. For a unique experience, venture underground to explore the mesmerizing limestone caves, such as Mammoth Cave and Lake Cave, adorned with impressive stalactites and stalagmites.

The coastline of the Margaret River Region is a treasure trove of pristine beaches. From popular surfing spots like Surfers Point and Yallingup Beach to tranquil bays like Hamelin Bay and Meelup Beach, there is a beach to suit every taste. Don't miss the chance to witness the majestic whales that migrate along the coast between June and November. Take a whale-watching tour to catch a glimpse of these magnificent creatures in their natural habitat.

2. World-Class Wineries and Gastronomic Delights

The Margaret River Region has earned a well-deserved reputation as one of Australia's premier wine regions. With over 200 vineyards and more than 100 world-class wineries, wine enthusiasts are in for a treat. Embark on a wine tasting journey, visiting renowned wineries such as Vasse Felix, Leeuwin Estate, and Cullen Wines, known for their exceptional vintages. Indulge in cellar door tastings, where you can savor the region's signature varietals, including Cabernet Sauvignon, Chardonnay, and Semillon Sauvignon Blanc.

Beyond its wineries, the Margaret River Region is a food lover's paradise, boasting a vibrant culinary scene. Sample the region's fresh produce at the bustling farmers' markets, where you can pick up locally grown fruits, vegetables, artisanal cheeses, and organic meats. Treat your taste buds to exquisite dining experiences at the region's award-winning restaurants, showcasing the finest regional ingredients. Don't miss the chance to savor the famous Margaret River marron, a local freshwater crayfish, or indulge in the delectable chocolates and truffles crafted by talented chocolatiers.

3. Outdoor Adventures and Thrilling Activities

For adventure seekers and outdoor enthusiasts, the Margaret River Region offers an array of thrilling activities. The region's coastline is renowned for its fantastic surf breaks, attracting surfers from around the world. Whether you're a seasoned pro or a beginner, there are surf schools and surf spots suitable for all skill levels. Immerse yourself in the surf culture and catch a wave at renowned breaks like Prevelly, Injidup, or Margaret River Main Break.

If you prefer to explore the region's waterways, embark on a kayaking or stand-up paddleboarding adventure along the tranquil

Margaret River. Paddle through the serene waters, surrounded by lush vegetation and abundant birdlife. For a more exhilarating experience, try your hand at kiteboarding or windsurfing, harnessing the region's winds for an adrenaline-fueled ride.

4. Arts, Culture, and Festivals

Beyond its natural wonders, the Margaret River Region is also a thriving hub of arts and culture. Explore the vibrant art galleries and studios, showcasing the works of talented local artists. From traditional Aboriginal art to contemporary sculptures and paintings, there is a diverse range of artistic expressions to discover.

The region hosts a variety of cultural events and festivals throughout the year, providing visitors with a unique opportunity to immerse themselves in the local arts scene. The Margaret River Gourmet Escape, held annually in November, is a food and wine extravaganza that attracts renowned chefs and food enthusiasts from around the world. The Augusta River Festival celebrates the region's maritime heritage, featuring boat races, live music, and delicious seafood. Whether you're interested in music, literature, or visual arts, there is always something happening in the Margaret River Region to satisfy your cultural cravings.

The Margaret River Region, with its stunning natural landscapes, world-class wineries, and thriving arts and culinary scene, is a captivating destination that should be on every traveler's bucket list. Whether you're seeking outdoor adventures, indulgent wine tastings, or a serene escape in nature, this region has it all. Immerse yourself in the beauty of the towering karri forests, explore the hidden limestone caves, and unwind on the pristine beaches. Discover the artistry of the region's winemakers, savor the flavors of its local produce, and immerse yourself in its vibrant arts and cultural scene.

When planning your visit to the Margaret River Region, consider the best time to travel, which is during the mild spring and autumn seasons when the weather is pleasant, and the crowds are fewer. Ensure you have ample time to explore the vast offerings of the region and consider booking accommodations in advance, as it can get busy during peak travel periods.

Embark on a journey to the Margaret River Region, where you can create memories that will last a lifetime. Whether you're a nature enthusiast, wine connoisseur, or adventure seeker, this captivating region in Western Australia promises an unforgettable experience that showcases the best of Australian hospitality and natural beauty.

• Outdoor Activities and Wildlife

Perth, the capital city of Western Australia, is renowned for its stunning natural beauty, abundant wildlife, and a myriad of outdoor activities. Nestled along the pristine coastline of the Indian Ocean, Perth offers a perfect blend of urban sophistication and untamed wilderness. With its favorable climate and diverse landscapes, Western Australia is a haven for nature enthusiasts and adventure seekers alike. In this comprehensive travel guide, we will explore the incredible outdoor activities and wildlife encounters that await you in Perth and throughout Western Australia.

1. Exploring Perth's Natural Wonders

Perth is blessed with an array of natural wonders, starting with the enchanting Kings

Park and Botanic Garden. Spanning over 400 hectares, this urban oasis showcases native flora, sweeping views of the city skyline, and the iconic Swan River. Enjoy leisurely walks, picnics, and guided tours while immersing yourself in Western Australia's unique biodiversity.

For a beach lover's paradise, head to Cottesloe Beach or Scarborough Beach, where golden sands meet crystal-clear waters. These beaches offer opportunities for swimming, surfing, snorkeling, or simply basking in the sun. Additionally, Rottnest Island, just a short ferry ride from Perth, is a must-visit destination. Encounter adorable quokkas, cycle around the island, snorkel in turquoise waters, and explore historic landmarks.

2. Wildlife Encounters in Western Australia

Western Australia boasts an incredible array of wildlife, both on land and in the ocean. One of the most sought-after wildlife encounters is swimming with the gentle giants of the sea, whale sharks. Ningaloo Reef, a UNESCO World Heritage Site, offers unforgettable snorkeling and diving experiences, where you can swim alongside these magnificent creatures during their annual migration.

Further north, the remote Kimberley region provides an opportunity to witness the awe-inspiring spectacle of the Horizontal Falls, where powerful tidal currents create a natural phenomenon. Explore the region's diverse ecosystem, home to crocodiles, turtles, and rare bird species.

Inland, the World Heritage-listed Purnululu National Park is famous for the Bungle Bungle Range. Embark on scenic hikes through the striking beehive-shaped rock formations and discover the park's unique wildlife, including wallabies, echidnas, and an array of birdlife.

3. Adventure Sports and Outdoor Activities

Western Australia's rugged terrain and vast landscapes offer endless opportunities for adventure sports and outdoor activities. Thrill-seekers can indulge in skydiving, sandboarding, and four-wheel driving on the expansive sand dunes of Lancelin or the Pinnacles Desert. For a unique experience, take a scenic flight over the extraordinary Wave Rock, a giant rock formation resembling an ocean wave frozen in time.

Nature enthusiasts can explore the magnificent gorges and waterfalls of Karijini National Park in the Pilbara region. Hiking trails take you deep into ancient geological formations, where you can swim in natural rock pools and marvel at the park's stunning scenery.

If you're seeking an off-road adventure, head to the Gibb River Road in the Kimberley region. This iconic outback route showcases breathtaking landscapes, secluded swimming holes, and opportunities for bush camping under the starlit sky.

4. National Parks and Conservation Areas

Western Australia boasts an extensive network of national parks and conservation areas, preserving its unique flora and fauna. Experience the wonder of nature at the Fitzgerald River National Park, a UNESCO Biosphere Reserve, home to over 1,800 plant species and numerous wildlife species, including the rare western ground parrot.

For a truly remote wilderness experience, venture to the remote Cape Range National Park. Snorkel or dive among vibrant coral reefs at the world-class Ningaloo Marine Park, where encounters with manta rays, turtles, and dugongs are common.

The vast and ancient Karri forests of the South West offer tranquil walks and scenic drives. Don't miss the Valley of the Giants, where you can walk among towering tingle trees on a suspended treetop walkway.

Perth and Western Australia are a haven for outdoor enthusiasts and wildlife lovers. From the breathtaking landscapes of Kings Park and Botanic Garden to the captivating encounters with whale sharks at Ningaloo Reef, Western Australia offers an array of unforgettable experiences. Whether you're seeking adventure sports, wildlife encounters, or serene natural beauty, this region has it all. Immerse yourself in the wonders of nature, explore the national parks, and revel in the rich biodiversity that makes Western Australia a true paradise for nature enthusiasts. Pack your bags and embark on an unforgettable journey to Perth and Western Australia, where outdoor adventures and wildlife encounters await at every turn.

• *Wine and Food Experiences*

Perth, the capital city of Western Australia, is a hidden gem when it comes to wine and food experiences. The region boasts a vibrant culinary scene that showcases the best of Australian produce, combined with world-class wineries and breathtaking vineyard landscapes. From the Swan Valley to the Margaret River region, this travel guide will take you on a gastronomic journey through Perth and Western Australia, exploring the diverse flavors, exquisite wines, and unforgettable culinary adventures.

1. Swan Valley:

Located just a short drive from Perth's city center, the Swan Valley is Western Australia's oldest wine region, renowned for its boutique wineries, picturesque vineyards, and gourmet food offerings. Visitors can embark on wine tours and tastings, exploring award-winning wineries such as Sandalford, Houghton, and Lancaster Wines. Indulge in a leisurely lunch overlooking the vineyards, where you can savor local delicacies and seasonal produce at renowned establishments like the Swan Valley Café or the historic Mandoon Estate.

2. Margaret River:

Venturing further south, the Margaret River region is a must-visit destination for wine enthusiasts and foodies alike. With over 120 wineries, the region produces some of Australia's finest wines, particularly renowned for its Cabernet Sauvignon and Chardonnay. Notable wineries to explore include Leeuwin Estate, Voyager Estate, and Vasse Felix. The

Margaret River Gourmet Escape, an annual food and wine festival, attracts visitors from around the world to experience the region's culinary delights.

3. Wine and Food Festivals:

Perth and Western Australia host a myriad of wine and food festivals throughout the year. In addition to the Margaret River Gourmet Escape, other notable events include the Perth Wine Festival, the Fremantle Food and Wine Festival, and the Taste Great Southern festival. These festivals showcase the region's diverse food and wine offerings, featuring celebrity chefs, cooking demonstrations, wine tastings, and local produce markets.

4. Farm-to-Table Experiences:

Western Australia's vast landscapes and fertile soil provide the perfect conditions for a thriving farm-to-table movement. Many restaurants and cafes in Perth and the surrounding regions source their ingredients locally, offering fresh, seasonal produce in their menus. Visit places like Bib & Tucker or Wildflower, which highlight indigenous ingredients and embrace sustainable culinary practices. For a truly immersive experience, consider visiting local farms and orchards to learn about the production process and even pick your own fruits or vegetables.

5. Indigenous Culinary Experiences:

Exploring the native flavors of Western Australia is an essential part of any food and wine journey in the region. Indigenous culinary experiences provide insights into Aboriginal culture, traditions, and the unique ingredients of the land. Engage in bush tucker tours, where knowledgeable guides introduce you to native plants, herbs, and spices. Join a Dreamtime story-telling dinner or participate in a traditional Aboriginal cooking class to understand the deep connection between food and the Aboriginal people.

6. Coastal Delights:

Perth's coastal location allows for an abundance of fresh seafood offerings. Visit the iconic Fishing Boat Harbour in Fremantle, where you can enjoy freshly caught fish and chips, or indulge in exquisite seafood platters at restaurants like Cicerello's or Kailis' Fish Market Café. For a more unique experience, take a seafood cruise to catch your own crayfish or embark on a coastal foraging tour to discover edible treasures along the shoreline.

7. Craft Beer and Distilleries:

Beyond wine, Perth and Western Australia are also home to a thriving craft beer and distillery scene. Microbreweries and distilleries have sprung up throughout the region, producing a wide range of unique and flavorsome beverages. Sample local craft beers at breweries like Little Creatures or Feral Brewing Company, or explore the world of spirits at distilleries such as Whipper Snapper Distillery or Great Southern Distilling Company.

Perth and Western Australia offer an extraordinary blend of wine, food, and culinary experiences that cater to all tastes and preferences. Whether you're a wine connoisseur, a food enthusiast, or simply seeking an unforgettable gastronomic adventure, this region has it all. From the world-class wineries of the Swan Valley and Margaret River to the diverse farm-to-table experiences, indigenous culinary delights, coastal seafood, and craft beer and distillery scene, Perth and Western Australia are a food and wine lover's paradise. So, come immerse yourself in the flavors of Western Australia and create memories that will last a lifetime.

• *Arts and Culture*

Perth and Western Australia, located on the western coast of Australia, offer a captivating blend of natural beauty and thriving arts and cultural scenes. From world-class museums and galleries to vibrant festivals and events, this region boasts a rich tapestry of artistic expression. In this Australia travel guide, we will delve into the diverse arts and culture of Perth and Western Australia, highlighting the key attractions, events, and venues that make this region a haven for art enthusiasts and cultural explorers.

1. *Museums and Galleries:*

Perth is home to an array of exceptional museums and galleries that showcase both local and international art. The Art Gallery of Western Australia, situated in the heart of Perth's cultural precinct, displays a comprehensive collection of Australian and Indigenous artworks, spanning various periods and styles. Visitors can admire works by renowned artists such as Sidney Nolan and Albert Namatjira.

The Western Australian Museum, located in the stunning heritage-listed buildings of the Perth Cultural Centre, is a treasure trove of natural history, cultural heritage, and contemporary art. Its diverse exhibits feature everything from ancient fossils and indigenous artifacts to modern installations and interactive displays.

Fremantle, a charming port city just south of Perth, houses the Fremantle Arts Centre, housed in a historic building dating back to the 1860s. This center hosts contemporary art exhibitions, artist residencies, and workshops, providing a platform for emerging and established artists to showcase their talent.

2. Indigenous Culture:

Western Australia is home to a rich and ancient Indigenous culture. Exploring and appreciating Indigenous art and traditions is an integral part of experiencing the region's cultural heritage. The Perth Cultural Centre is home to the Western Australian Indigenous Art Awards, an annual exhibition that celebrates the artistic achievements of Aboriginal and Torres Strait Islander artists.

Travelers can also visit the Aboriginal Art Gallery in Kings Park, where they can view and purchase authentic Indigenous artworks, including paintings, sculptures, and artifacts. Additionally, the Wardandi Boodja Cultural Tours in Margaret River offer immersive experiences, allowing visitors to learn about the local Noongar people's culture, traditions, and connection to the land.

3. Festivals and Events:

Perth and Western Australia host a multitude of vibrant festivals and events throughout the year, showcasing various art forms and cultural expressions. The Perth Festival, held annually in February, is one of Australia's premier cultural events, featuring an exciting program of theater, music, dance, film, and visual arts. The festival brings together local, national, and international artists, captivating audiences with its diverse and thought-provoking performances.

The Revelation Perth International Film Festival, held in July, is a celebration of independent and alternative cinema. It showcases a range of films, including documentaries, short films, and experimental works, offering a unique and immersive cinematic experience.

Other notable events include the Margaret River Gourmet Escape, a food and wine festival that combines culinary delights with art and music, and the Sculpture by the Sea exhibition in Cottesloe, where stunning sculptures adorn the beachfront, creating an extraordinary outdoor gallery.

4. Performing Arts:

Perth boasts a vibrant performing arts scene, with a range of theaters, opera houses, and concert halls showcasing world-class productions. The Perth Concert Hall is a renowned venue that hosts symphony concerts, ballet performances, and opera productions. The State Theatre Centre of Western Australia is a hub for contemporary theater, hosting a diverse range of local and international productions.

For those seeking innovative and experimental performances, the Blue Room Theatre in Perth's cultural precinct is a must-visit. It supports emerging artists and showcases boundary-pushing works across various genres, including theater, dance, and live art.

5. Street Art and Public Installations:

Perth's streets and laneways are adorned with vibrant street art and captivating public installations. The Perth Cultural Centre features numerous murals and sculptures, with each artwork telling a unique story. Northbridge, a bustling entertainment district, is a haven for street art enthusiasts, with its laneways and walls serving as canvases for local and international artists.

The FORM Public Art Trail in the Perth CBD showcases a series of thought-provoking sculptures and installations that engage with the urban landscape and encourage public interaction. Exploring these outdoor art spaces provides a unique opportunity to discover Perth's urban art scene.

Perth and Western Australia offer an enticing blend of artistic expression, cultural heritage, and natural beauty. With its world-class museums and galleries, thriving festivals and events, and diverse performing arts scene, the region provides a rich and immersive cultural experience. Whether it's exploring Indigenous art, witnessing captivating performances, or admiring vibrant street art, Perth and Western Australia are a treasure trove for art and culture enthusiasts. So, immerse yourself in this captivating region and let the arts and culture of Perth and Western Australia inspire and delight you.

CHAPTER EIGHT

Adelaide and South Australia

• *Overview of Adelaide and South Australia*

Nestled on the southern coast of Australia, Adelaide, the capital city of South Australia, offers an enchanting blend of cultural heritage, stunning landscapes, and a vibrant cosmopolitan atmosphere. With its charming wine regions, pristine beaches, and diverse wildlife, South Australia offers an unforgettable travel experience for adventurers, nature enthusiasts, and food lovers alike. In this comprehensive travel guide, we will explore the highlights of Adelaide and South Australia, delving into their rich history, natural wonders, unique attractions, and culinary delights.

I. History and Culture:

A. Indigenous Heritage: South Australia has a rich Indigenous history, with numerous Aboriginal nations having inhabited the region for thousands of years. Visitors can explore Aboriginal cultural sites, engage in guided tours, and gain insights into the ancient Dreamtime stories and traditions.

B. Colonial Legacy: Adelaide was founded in 1836 as a planned British colony, and its layout reflects the influence of British town planning. The city's historic precincts, such as North Terrace, offer glimpses into the colonial past through beautifully preserved buildings, museums, and art galleries.

C. Festivals and Arts: Adelaide is renowned for its vibrant arts scene, hosting various festivals throughout the year. The Adelaide Festival, Adelaide Fringe, and WOMADelaide attract artists and performers from around the globe, making the city a hub of creativity and cultural diversity.

II. Natural Wonders:
A. The Barossa Valley: Located just an hour's drive from Adelaide, the Barossa Valley is one of Australia's premier wine regions. Visitors can indulge in wine tastings, cellar door

experiences, and explore the picturesque vineyards, which produce world-class Shiraz and other renowned varietals.

B. Kangaroo Island: A short ferry ride from the mainland, Kangaroo Island offers a sanctuary for unique wildlife and pristine landscapes. Visitors can spot kangaroos, koalas, sea lions, and even penguins in their natural habitats, while also enjoying the island's rugged coastline, stunning beaches, and breathtaking rock formations.

C. Flinders Ranges: Venture further north to the ancient Flinders Ranges, where dramatic mountain ranges, deep gorges, and red earth create a stunning natural backdrop. Hiking trails, Aboriginal rock art sites, and the iconic Wilpena Pound make it a paradise for nature lovers and outdoor enthusiasts.

III. Coastal Escapes:
A. Adelaide's Beaches: With a coastline stretching over 3,800 kilometers, South Australia is blessed with an array of beautiful beaches. From the lively Glenelg Beach, with its bustling promenade, to the tranquil shores of Semaphore and Henley Beach, visitors can relax, swim, and soak up the sun.

B. Eyre Peninsula: Known as Australia's seafood frontier, the Eyre Peninsula boasts pristine coastal scenery, abundant marine life, and delicious seafood offerings. From cage diving with great white sharks to swimming with playful sea lions, the region offers thrilling aquatic adventures for the adventurous traveler.

C. Fleurieu Peninsula: Just a short drive from Adelaide, the Fleurieu Peninsula is a haven for wine lovers, surfers, and nature enthusiasts. The McLaren Vale wine region, picturesque coastal towns like Victor Harbor, and the stunning cliffs of the Deep Creek Conservation Park are highlights of this coastal paradise.

IV. Gastronomic Delights:
A. Adelaide Central Market: Immerse yourself in the culinary delights of Adelaide at the bustling Central Market, where local produce, gourmet delights, and multicultural flavors abound. Sample artisan cheeses, freshly caught seafood, exotic spices, and indulge in diverse cuisines from around the world.

B. Wine and Food Trails: South Australia's wine regions, including the Barossa Valley,

McLaren Vale, and ClareValley, offer not only world-class wines but also delectable food experiences. Enjoy a long lunch at a vineyard restaurant, savoring regional specialties paired with the perfect wine.

C. Seafood Feast: With a coastline teeming with seafood, South Australia is a seafood lover's paradise. From succulent oysters from Coffin Bay to the famous blue swimmer crabs of Port Lincoln, indulge in the freshest catch and culinary delights from the ocean.

Adelaide and South Australia offer a diverse range of experiences that cater to every traveler's interests. From exploring the city's rich history and cultural heritage to immersing oneself in the stunning natural wonders and indulging in world-class food and wine, this region is a treasure trove of experiences waiting to be discovered. Whether you're an adventure seeker, a nature lover, or a food enthusiast, Adelaide and South Australia will leave you with unforgettable memories and a deep appreciation for the beauty and diversity of Australia's landscapes and cultures.

• *Top Attractions*

Located in the southern region of Australia, Adelaide and its surrounding state of South Australia offer an array of captivating attractions that showcase the country's natural beauty, rich history, and vibrant culture. From picturesque coastal landscapes and world-renowned wine regions to fascinating wildlife encounters and cultural landmarks, this comprehensive travel guide will highlight the top attractions that make Adelaide and South Australia an enticing destination for travelers. So, let's embark on an unforgettable journey through this captivating part of Australia.

I. Adelaide City:

1. Adelaide Oval: Begin your exploration in the heart of Adelaide at the iconic Adelaide Oval, a premier sports and entertainment venue with a history dating back to 1871. Take a guided tour to learn about its remarkable architecture and immerse yourself in the vibrant atmosphere during live sporting events.

2. Adelaide Central Market: Experience the bustling atmosphere of the Adelaide Central Market, a food lover's paradise that has been delighting visitors since 1869. Stroll through

the stalls, savor local produce, and indulge in gourmet treats from around the world.

3. North Terrace Cultural Precinct: Discover Adelaide's cultural treasures along North Terrace, where you'll find the South Australian Museum, Art Gallery of South Australia, and the State Library of South Australia. Explore diverse art collections, delve into Aboriginal and natural history, and enrich your knowledge of the region's heritage.

4. Adelaide Botanic Garden: Escape to nature within the city limits at the Adelaide Botanic Garden. Explore the stunningly landscaped grounds, wander through themed gardens, and visit the iconic Bicentennial Conservatory, home to an impressive array of exotic plants.

II. Coastal Escapes:

1. Glenelg: Just a short tram ride from Adelaide, Glenelg offers a beautiful sandy beach, vibrant shopping precincts, and a lively entertainment scene. Enjoy a leisurely stroll along the jetty, take a dip in the turquoise waters, or indulge in delicious seafood at one of the beachfront restaurants.

2. Kangaroo Island: A short ferry ride from the mainland, Kangaroo Island is a nature lover's paradise. Witness diverse wildlife in their natural habitat, including kangaroos, koalas, sea lions, and vibrant bird species. Explore stunning coastal landscapes, pristine beaches, and unique rock formations.

3. Fleurieu Peninsula: Boasting stunning coastal scenery and world-class wineries, the Fleurieu Peninsula is a haven for food and wine enthusiasts. Explore the picturesque coastal towns of Victor Harbor and Port Elliot, sample local wines in McLaren Vale, and marvel at the breathtaking vistas along the rugged coastline.

III. Wine Regions:

1. Barossa Valley: Indulge in the world-famous wines of the Barossa Valley, one of Australia's most renowned wine regions. Embark on a wine tour, visit historic cellar doors, and savor the rich flavors of Shiraz, Grenache, and other varietals. Don't miss the chance to dine at award-winning restaurants and immerse yourself in the region's culinary delights.

2. Clare Valley: Known for its boutique wineries and charming countryside, the Clare Valley offers a more intimate wine-tasting

experience. Explore the picturesque vineyards, meet passionate winemakers, and sample elegant Rieslings and full-bodied reds in this tranquil setting.

3. Adelaide Hills: A short drive from Adelaide, the Adelaide Hills region offers a delightful blend of cool-climate wines, quaint villages, and breathtaking landscapes. Visit cellar doors nestled among rolling hills, taste exceptional cool-climate wines, and enjoy the region's thriving food scene.

IV. Natural Wonders:
1. Flinders Ranges: Venture into the rugged beauty of the Flinders Ranges, where ancient landscapes, dramaticgorges, and breathtaking mountain ranges await. Take scenic hikes through Wilpena Pound, witness Aboriginal rock art, and immerse yourself in the rich cultural heritage of the Adnyamathanha people.

2. Eyre Peninsula: Renowned for its pristine coastline and abundant marine life, the Eyre Peninsula offers incredible opportunities for diving, swimming with sea lions, and even shark cage diving. Explore the stunning beaches of Coffin Bay, taste fresh oysters, and

encounter dolphins and whales in their natural habitat.

3. Kangaroo Island Wildlife: Get up close and personal with iconic Australian wildlife on Kangaroo Island. Visit Seal Bay Conservation Park to observe sea lions in their natural environment, marvel at the playful antics of Kangaroo Island's resident penguins, and spot kangaroos, koalas, and echidnas in their natural habitats.

Adelaide and South Australia encompass a remarkable blend of vibrant city life, stunning coastal escapes, renowned wine regions, and awe-inspiring natural wonders. Whether you're a nature enthusiast, wine connoisseur, or culture seeker, this captivating part of Australia offers an abundance of experiences to satisfy every traveler's desires. Embrace the warmth of the locals, savor exquisite culinary delights, and create lifelong memories as you explore the top attractions of Adelaide and South Australia.

Adelaide Central Market

Located in the heart of Adelaide, South Australia, the Adelaide Central Market is a bustling and vibrant culinary destination that has been captivating locals and visitors for over a century. With its rich history, diverse range of produce, and lively atmosphere, the market stands as a testament to the region's thriving food culture. This serves as a comprehensive travel guide, offering an in-depth exploration of the Adelaide Central Market and its significance in the Australian culinary landscape.

1. Historical Background:

The Adelaide Central Market dates back to 1869 when it first opened its doors to the public. Established as a result of growing demand for fresh food in the expanding city, the market quickly became a hub for local producers and traders. Over the years, it has evolved to become one of the largest undercover markets in the Southern Hemisphere, spanning over 8,000 square meters and accommodating over 80 stalls. Despite its long history, the market has managed to retain its authentic charm and continues to be a beloved institution among locals.

2. Unique Market Experience:

Stepping into the Adelaide Central Market is like immersing oneself in a sensory feast. The market's vibrant atmosphere is fueled by the lively chatter of traders, the enticing aromas of freshly baked goods, and the vibrant colors of seasonal produce. Visitors can expect to find an extensive array of products, ranging from fresh fruits, vegetables, and seafood to specialty cheeses, meats, and baked goods. The market is also home to a variety of cafes, eateries, and specialty stores, offering a diverse range of cuisines and culinary delights.

3. Local Produce and Artisanal Products:

One of the defining features of the Adelaide Central Market is its emphasis on locally sourced and seasonal produce. South Australia's fertile soil and temperate climate contribute to the region's abundance of high-quality fruits, vegetables, and grains. The market showcases the best of these offerings, with vendors proudly displaying their fresh produce and engaging in conversations with customers. Additionally, the market is a treasure trove of artisanal products, including homemade jams, preserves, chocolates, and small-batch wines. These products reflect the passion and dedication of local producers and provide visitors with an opportunity to support sustainable and ethical practices.

4. Culinary Delights:

The Adelaide Central Market is a haven for food lovers, offering an extensive range of culinary delights from around the world. The market's multicultural influence is evident in the diverse range of cuisines available, including Italian, Greek, Asian, Middle Eastern, and more. Whether visitors are craving a hearty pasta dish, traditional Greek souvlaki, or exotic flavors from the Far East, they are sure to find a stall or eatery that caters to their taste buds. The market also hosts cooking demonstrations, allowing visitors to learn from talented chefs and gain insights into various culinary techniques.

5. Events and Festivities:

Throughout the year, the Adelaide Central Market plays host to a series of events and festivities that celebrate food, culture, and community. From cooking classes and wine tastings to seasonal festivals and live music performances, there is always something happening at the market. One of the most popular events is the annual CheeseFest, where cheese enthusiasts gather to sample a wide selection of artisanal cheeses and learn from industry experts. These events add an extra layer of excitement and make the market a vibrant and dynamic destination for both locals and tourists.

6. Supporting Local Businesses:

Visiting the Adelaide Central Market is not just about experiencing a delightful culinary journey; it is also an opportunity to support local businesses and artisans. Many of the vendors at the market are small-scale producers who rely on the market as their primary avenue for selling their products. By purchasing directly from these vendors, visitors contribute to the sustainability of local agriculture and help preserve traditional food practices. Moreover, engaging in conversations with vendors and learning about their stories adds a personal touch to the market experience, creating a sense of connection and community.

The Adelaide Central Market is a testament to the rich culinary heritage of South Australia and a must-visit destination for food enthusiasts. Its vibrant atmosphere, diverse range of produce, and commitment to supporting local businesses make it a standout market in the Australian landscape. From fresh produce to artisanal products, from multicultural cuisines to lively events, the market offers an unforgettable experience that tantalizes the senses and fosters a deeper appreciation for the culinary arts. Whether you are a local looking for a taste of home or a visitor seeking an authentic food experience, the Adelaide Central Market is sure to leave a lasting impression.

Barossa Valley

Barossa Valley, nestled in the heart of Adelaide and South Australia, is a captivating destination for wine enthusiasts, nature lovers, and those seeking a relaxing getaway. Renowned for its world-class vineyards, picturesque landscapes, and rich cultural heritage, Barossa Valley offers a unique and immersive travel experience. This comprehensive travel guide will delve into the charms of Barossa Valley, providing insights into its wine regions, attractions, gastronomy, and the best ways to make the most of your visit.

1. Location and Accessibility:

Barossa Valley is located just 60 kilometers northeast of Adelaide, the vibrant capital city of South Australia. Travelers can easily reach Barossa Valley by car, making it an ideal day trip from Adelaide. The journey takes approximately one hour, and the scenic drive offers breathtaking views of the region's rolling hills and vineyards. Alternatively, several tour operators provide guided tours to Barossa Valley, offering hassle-free transportation and expert insights along the way.

2. Wine Regions and Vineyards:

Barossa Valley is home to some of Australia's oldest and most prestigious vineyards, making it a wine lover's paradise. There are two main wine regions within Barossa Valley: the Barossa Valley region and the Eden Valley region.

- Barossa Valley Region: Known for its bold and full-bodied red wines, the Barossa Valley region boasts iconic wineries such as Penfolds, Seppeltsfield, and Henschke. Visitors can indulge in wine tastings, cellar door experiences, and guided tours to learn about the winemaking process, sample premium vintages, and purchase their favorite bottles.

- Eden Valley Region: Situated in the elevated eastern ranges of Barossa Valley, the Eden Valley region is renowned for its cool climate wines, particularly Riesling and Shiraz. Wineries such as Henschke's Hill of Grace and Yalumba showcase the region's unique terroir, offering visitors a chance to savor exceptional cool-climate varietals.

3. Attractions and Activities:
Aside from its exquisite vineyards, Barossa Valley offers a plethora of attractions and activities to suit every traveler's interests. Here are some highlights:

- Mengler Hill Lookout: For breathtaking panoramic views of Barossa Valley, head to Mengler Hill Lookout. This vantage point provides an ideal spot to admire the undulating vineyards, patchwork fields, and the valley's natural beauty.

- Barossa Farmers Market: Immerse yourself in the vibrant local food scene by visiting the

Barossa Farmers Market. Held every Saturday, the market showcases an array of fresh produce, artisanal food products, and local delicacies.

- Maggie Beer's Farm Shop: Food enthusiasts should not miss the opportunity to visit Maggie Beer's Farm Shop. Sample gourmet delights, including pâtés, preserves, and ice creams, all made from the finest Barossa Valley ingredients.

- Balloon Rides: Take to the skies and experience Barossa Valley's enchanting landscapes from a hot air balloon. Drifting over the vineyards during sunrise or sunset offers a truly magical and unforgettable experience.

4. Cultural Heritage and Festivals:
Barossa Valley's rich cultural heritage is deeply intertwined with its wine industry. The region is home to many German settlers who brought their winemaking expertise, traditions, and architecture to the area. Explore the charming town of Tanunda, visit historic churches, and marvel at the traditional German-style cottages.

The Barossa Vintage Festival, held biennially, is a celebration of the region's wine, food, and cultural heritage. It offers a diverse program of events, including wine tastings, culinary experiences, parades, and live performances. The festival attracts visitors from around the globe, providing an opportunity to immerse oneself in Barossa Valley's vibrant atmosphere.

5. Gastronomy and Dining:

Barossa Valley's culinary scene is as diverse and delightful as its wines. From fine dining establishments to rustic cellar doors, the region offers a plethora of gastronomic experiences. Indulge in locally sourced produce, farm-to-table dishes, and innovative menus showcasing the best of Barossa Valley's flavors.

- Regional Cuisine: Try traditional German-inspired dishes, such as bratwurst, sauerkraut, and pretzels, at local restaurants and pubs. Don't forget to pair your meal with a glass of Barossa Valley's finest wine.

- Long Table Dining: Experience the conviviality of long table dining, where visitors come together to savor a shared meal in a picturesque vineyard setting. This unique culinary experience fosters a sense of community while enjoying delicious local fare.

- Cooking Classes: Enhance your culinary skills by participating in a cooking class led by renowned chefs. Learn the secrets behind regional recipes and gain insights into food and wine pairings.

Barossa Valley, a wine lover's haven nestled in Adelaide and South Australia, offers an enchanting journey through its vineyards, attractions, gastronomy, and cultural heritage. With its exceptional wines, stunning landscapes, and warm hospitality, this captivating destination guarantees an unforgettable travel experience. Whether you're a wine enthusiast, a food lover, or a nature seeker, Barossa Valley invites you to indulge in its charms and create lasting memories. Plan your visit to Barossa Valley, and embark on an extraordinary adventure in Australia's wine wonderland.

Kangaroo Island

Nestled off the coast of South Australia, Kangaroo Island is an enchanting gem and a must-visit destination for travelers exploring Australia. Known for its pristine wilderness, diverse wildlife, stunning landscapes, and warm hospitality, Kangaroo Island offers a unique experience that is hard to find anywhere else in the world. This comprehensive travel guide will take you on a journey through the wonders of Kangaroo Island and its connection to Adelaide and South Australia. From its history and natural beauty to its activities and attractions, we will delve deep into this extraordinary island paradise.

1. A Brief History

Kangaroo Island has a rich history that dates back thousands of years, with Aboriginal people having lived on the island for at least 16,000 years. The local Kaurna and Ramindjeri people are the traditional custodians of the land and have maintained their connection to the island through their culture and stories.

European exploration of the island began in the early 19th century when British navigator Matthew Flinders mapped its coastline. He encountered numerous kangaroos and decided to name the island "Kangaroo Island." Since then, European settlers arrived on the island, engaging in industries such as agriculture and fishing.

2. How to Get to Kangaroo Island

Kangaroo Island is accessible from Adelaide, the capital city of South Australia. Travelers have two primary options to reach the island:

a. By Ferry: SeaLink operates regular ferries between the mainland and Kangaroo Island. The ferry departs from Cape Jervis, approximately 110 kilometers south of Adelaide, and arrives at Penneshaw, Kangaroo Island's main town. The ferry ride is a scenic journey that takes around 45 minutes and offers breathtaking views of the coastline.

b. By Air: For a quicker option, travelers can take a domestic flight from Adelaide Airport to Kingscote Airport on Kangaroo Island. Regional airlines like Regional Express (REX) offer regular flights, and the journey takes approximately 30 minutes.

3. Best Time to Visit

Kangaroo Island's climate is relatively mild, making it an ideal year-round destination. However, to make the most of your visit, consider the following seasons:

a. Spring (September - November):Spring brings pleasant weather with blooming wildflowers and baby animals. It's a fantastic time for nature walks and wildlife spotting.

b. Summer (December - February):The summer months offer warm temperatures, making it perfect for beach activities and water sports. Be prepared for higher visitor numbers during this period.

c. Autumn (March - May):The weather remains mild, and autumn colors create a picturesque backdrop for your explorations. It's also a great time to savor local produce and wines.

d. Winter (June - August):Winter brings cooler temperatures, but it's an excellent time for whale watching as Southern Right Whales migrate to the island's shores.

4. Where to Stay

Kangaroo Island offers a variety of accommodation options to suit every traveler's preferences and budget. From luxury resorts to cozy bed-and-breakfasts, you'll find a place that meets your needs.

a. Luxury Resorts:For a lavish experience, consider staying at one of the island's luxury resorts. They offer world-class amenities, stunning views, and access to exclusive experiences.

b. Eco-Lodges:Kangaroo Island takes pride in its commitment to sustainable tourism. Eco-lodges provide a unique opportunity to connect with nature while minimizing your environmental impact.

c. Self-Catering Accommodations:If you prefer a more independent stay, self-catering options like holiday homes and cottages

are available. They allow you to enjoy the comforts of home while exploring the island at your own pace.

d. Camping:For the adventurous souls, Kangaroo Island offers several camping sites where you can immerse yourself in nature. Just make sure to book in advance and familiarize yourself with the camping regulations.

5. Exploring Kangaroo Island

Once you've settled into your accommodation, it's time to embark on an adventure to explore the wonders of Kangaroo Island. Here are some of the island's top attractions and activities:

a. Flinders Chase National Park:Located on the western end of the island, Flinders Chase National Park is a haven for nature enthusiasts. Explore the Remarkable Rocks, Admirals Arch, and stroll along the numerous walking trails that lead you through untouched wilderness.

b. Seal Bay Conservation Park:A visit to Kangaroo Island wouldn't be complete without observing the island's most famous residents: Australian sea lions. Take a guided tour and witness these majestic creatures in their natural habitat.

c. Remarkable Wildlife:*
Kangaroo Island is a wildlife lover's paradise. Encounter koalas, kangaroos, echidnas, and a variety of bird species in their natural habitats. The island also boasts a sanctuary dedicated to

the protection of endangered species like the Kangaroo Island dunnart.

d. Remarkable Rocks:These massive granite boulders, sculpted by wind and sea over centuries, stand proudly along the coastline. Marvel at their unique formations and capture stunning photographs.

e. Food and Wine Experiences: Kangaroo Island is renowned for its fresh produce, seafood, and world-class wines. Visit local farms, wineries, and gourmet restaurants to savor the island's culinary delights.

6. Adelaide and South Australia Connection

Adelaide, the gateway to Kangaroo Island, serves as an excellent base for your South Australian adventures. Known for its vibrant arts scene, cultural festivals, and diverse dining options, Adelaide is a city worth exploring before or after your Kangaroo Island visit.

South Australia, as a whole, offers a multitude of attractions and experiences. From the vineyards of the Barossa Valley to the rugged coastline of the Eyre Peninsula, there is much to discover. You can also explore the Outback wonders of the Flinders Ranges or dive into the underwater paradise of the Great Australian Bight.

Kangaroo Island is a destination that captivates the imagination and leaves a lasting impression on all who visit. With its untouched wilderness, unique wildlife encounters, and breathtaking landscapes, it offers an escape from the ordinary and a chance to reconnect with nature. Whether you're a wildlife enthusiast, a food and wine connoisseur, or simply seeking tranquility, Kangaroo Island has something for everyone. So, pack your bags, embark on an unforgettable journey, and let the magic of Kangaroo Island and South Australia unfold before your eyes.

• *Nature and Wildlife Experiences*

Australia is renowned for its stunning landscapes and diverse wildlife, offering a wealth of nature-based experiences for travelers. In particular, the city of Adelaide and the surrounding region of South Australia boast an array of breathtaking natural wonders and unique wildlife encounters. This travel guide will take you on a journey through the best nature and wildlife experiences in Adelaide and South Australia, providing valuable insights and recommendations to make the most of your visit.

1. Adelaide:

1.1 Adelaide Botanic Garden: Begin your nature exploration in the heart of Adelaide at the beautiful Adelaide Botanic Garden. Spanning over 125 acres, this tranquil oasis is home to an extensive collection of plant species from around the world. Explore the themed gardens, including the stunning Bicentennial Conservatory and the National Rose Trial Garden.

1.2 Cleland Wildlife Park: Just a short drive from Adelaide, Cleland Wildlife Park offers a unique opportunity to get up close and personal with Australia's iconic wildlife. Wander through the park and interact with kangaroos, koalas, and emus. Don't miss the chance to hold a koala or hand-feed kangaroos for an unforgettable experience.

1.3 Dolphin Sanctuary and Ships Graveyard: Embark on a scenic cruise to the Dolphin Sanctuary and Ships Graveyard located near

Adelaide's coastline. Witness playful dolphins in their natural habitat as they swim alongside the boat. Learn about the area's maritime history and explore the remains of ships that lie at the bottom of the ocean.

2. *Kangaroo Island:*

2.1 Flinders Chase National Park: Kangaroo Island, just a short ferry ride from Adelaide, is a haven for wildlife enthusiasts. Discover Flinders Chase National Park, home to impressive natural landmarks like Remarkable Rocks and Admirals Arch. Marvel at the rugged coastal scenery, spot kangaroos, wallabies, and koalas, and observe colonies of New Zealand fur seals.

2.2 Little Sahara: For a unique adventure, head to Little Sahara, a vast expanse of sand dunes perfect for sandboarding and exploring. Feel the adrenaline rush as you slide down the dunes or simply enjoy the stunning panoramic views.

2.3 Seal Bay Conservation Park: Visit Seal Bay Conservation Park to witness a colony of Australian sea lions in their natural environment. Join a guided tour and walk along the beach, observing these magnificent creatures basking in the sun or playing in the surf.

3. Eyre Peninsula:

3.1 Shark Cage Diving: Embark on an exhilarating adventure off the coast of Port Lincoln, known as the Great White Shark capital of Australia. Dive into the water in a cage to observe these awe-inspiring creatures up close, an experience that will leave you in awe of their power and beauty.

3.2 Coffin Bay National Park: Explore the pristine wilderness of Coffin Bay National Park, where rugged coastal landscapes meet tranquil beaches. Enjoy fishing, boating, bushwalking, or birdwatching in this untouched paradise.

3.3 Baird Bay: Swim with playful sea lions and dolphins in the crystal-clear waters of Baird Bay. Guided tours provide an unforgettable opportunity to interact with these intelligent creatures in their natural habitat.

4. The Flinders Ranges:

4.1 Wilpena Pound: Venture into the majestic Flinders Ranges and discover the natural amphitheater of Wilpena Pound. Hike through ancient gorges, gaze at towering rock formations, and marvel at the stunning panoramic views from the rim.

4.2 Arkaroola Wilderness Sanctuary: Immerse yourself in the rugged beauty of the Arkaroola Wilderness Sanctuary, a protected area known for its unique geological formations and abundance of wildlife. Take a 4WD tour, go stargazing, or embark on a bushwalk to fully appreciate the untouched wilderness.

Adelaide and South Australia offer an abundance of nature and wildlife experiences that will leave you captivated and inspired. From encounters with iconic Australian animals like kangaroos and koalas to breathtaking coastal scenery and outback adventures, this region promises unforgettable moments in the embrace of nature's wonders. Whether you choose to explore the city's gardens, venture to Kangaroo Island, dive with sharks, or hike through the Flinders Ranges, a visit to Adelaide and South Australia will undoubtedly ignite your sense of adventure and deepen your appreciation for the natural world.

• Food and Wine

Adelaide, the capital city of South Australia, is a true haven for food and wine enthusiasts. Nestled amidst picturesque landscapes, this region boasts a rich culinary heritage and a thriving wine industry. From world-class wineries to vibrant food markets and eclectic dining experiences, Adelaide and South Australia offer a gastronomic adventure like no other. In this travel guide, we will delve into the diverse culinary offerings, exquisite wines, and must-visit locations that make this region a paradise for food and wine lovers.

1. Adelaide Central Market:

A perfect starting point for any food lover, the Adelaide Central Market is a vibrant hub of culinary delights. Established in 1869, this iconic market is Australia's largest undercover fresh produce market. Here, you can explore an extensive range of fruits, vegetables, seafood, cheeses, and gourmet goods sourced from local producers. Immerse yourself in the lively atmosphere as you interact with passionate vendors and indulge in delicious street food offerings.

2. South Australian Seafood:

Located on the coast, South Australia is renowned for its exceptional seafood. The pristine waters of the Southern Ocean and Gulf St Vincent provide an abundance of fresh seafood varieties, including the famous King George Whiting, Coffin Bay oysters, Spencer Gulf prawns, and Southern Bluefin tuna. Visit renowned seafood restaurants in Adelaide, such as The Star of Greece in Port Willunga, to savor these culinary treasures.

3. Wine Regions of South Australia:
South Australia is home to some of the most celebrated wine regions in Australia, producing world-class wines that are recognized globally. The Barossa Valley, known for its robust Shiraz wines, offers picturesque vineyards and historic wineries. McLaren Vale, famous for its rich reds and Mediterranean climate, offers a relaxed wine-tasting experience. Other notable wine regions include Adelaide Hills, Clare Valley, Coonawarra, and the Limestone Coast. Embark on wine tours, indulge in cellar door tastings, and learn about the winemaking process while exploring these stunning regions.

4. Adelaide Hills Produce:
Nestled in the Mount Lofty Ranges, the Adelaide Hills region is a treasure trove of local

produce. The cool climate lends itself to the production of crisp cool-climate wines, apple and pear orchards, and boutique dairy products. Explore the charming town of Hahndorf, Australia's oldest surviving German settlement, where you can sample artisanal cheeses, freshly baked bread, and locally crafted chocolates. Don't miss the opportunity to visit the famous Beerenberg Farm, known for its delectable strawberry picking experiences.

5. Indigenous Culinary Heritage:
South Australia is also rich in Indigenous culinary heritage. Engage in unique food experiences that celebrate the traditional Aboriginal culture and its connection to the land. Join Aboriginal-led tours and learn about native bush foods, such as quandong, kangaroo, wattleseed, and saltbush. Discover traditional cooking techniques and taste the unique flavors at renowned Indigenous-owned restaurants like 'Ngeringa Cultural Centre' and 'Red Ochre Grill.'

6. Dining Experiences in Adelaide:
Adelaide boasts a thriving culinary scene with a plethora of dining options to suit all tastes and budgets. From high-end fine dining

establishments like Orana and Magill Estate to trendy laneway eateries serving international cuisines, there is something for everyone. Explore Gouger Street, known for its vibrant Asian eateries, or venture to Peel Street for an eclectic mix of cafes and bars. Don't forget to try the famous South Australian dessert, the Adelaide Central Market's iconic donut.

7. Festivals and Events:
Adelaide hosts a range of food and wine festivals throughout the year, celebrating the region's culinary diversity. The Tasting Australia festival is a highlight, showcasing the best produce, wines, and culinary talents from South Australia and around the country. The Cellar Door Fest, CheeseFest, and Sea & Vines Festival in McLaren Vale are also worth attending to immerse yourself in the local food and wine culture.

Adelaide and South Australia offer a captivating blend of flavors, aromas, and experiences for food and wine enthusiasts. From the bustling Central Market to the world-renowned wine regions, this region invites you on a gastronomic journey like no other. Immerse yourself in the culinary heritage, indulge in exceptional wines, and explore the diverse range of dining experiences that make Adelaide and South Australia an unmissable destination for any food and wine lover.

•Festivals and Events

Australia, the land of awe-inspiring landscapes and diverse cultural heritage, is a treasure trove of festivals and events. In the state of South Australia, the cosmopolitan city of Adelaide serves as a gateway to a kaleidoscope of festivities that celebrate art, culture, music, food, wine, and more. This travel guide invites you to explore the rich tapestry of festivals and events in Adelaide and South Australia, providing a glimpse into the vibrant spirit and unmatched hospitality of this region.

1. Adelaide Festival:
Kicking off the calendar of events in March, the Adelaide Festival sets the stage for an artistic extravaganza. With a captivating blend of international and local talent, this festival showcases a wide range of performances, including theatre, dance, music, and visual arts. The Adelaide Festival Parade, a vibrant

street procession, encapsulates the city's infectious energy.

2. WOMADelaide:

WOMADelaide, held annually in Botanic Park, brings together musicians and artists from across the globe for a celebration of world music, arts, and dance. This four-day festival offers an immersive cultural experience, complete with interactive workshops, delicious international cuisine, and a vibrant market.

3. Tasting Australia:

For food and wine enthusiasts, Tasting Australia is a gastronomic delight. Held biennially, this festival showcases South Australia's exceptional produce, culinary talent, and renowned wine regions. From gourmet dinners prepared by celebrity chefs to immersive food tours and masterclasses, Tasting Australia is a celebration of the region's rich culinary heritage.

4. Adelaide Fringe:

The Adelaide Fringe is the largest open-access arts festival in the Southern Hemisphere. Spanning four weeks from late February to mid-March, this festival transforms the city into a vibrant hub of creativity. Visitors can witness a diverse range of performances, including comedy, theatre, cabaret, circus, and visual arts, in venues ranging from theatres to pop-up spaces.

5. Santos Tour Down Under:

Cycling enthusiasts and sports lovers shouldn't miss the Santos Tour Down Under, the first event of the UCI WorldTour calendar. Held annually in January, this week-long festival attracts world-class cyclists who race through picturesque Adelaide Hills and stunning coastal routes. The event also includes family-friendly activities, community rides, and street parties.

6. Barossa Vintage Festival:

Nestled in South Australia's renowned wine region, the Barossa Vintage Festival is a celebration of the region's rich viticultural history. Held biennially, this festival offers visitors a chance to indulge in wine tastings, vineyard tours, gourmet feasts, and traditional German folk dancing. It's an immersive experience that showcases the Barossa's vibrant wine and food culture.

7. Sea and Vines Festival:

On the June long weekend, the McLaren Vale region comes alive with the Sea and Vines Festival. Wine connoisseurs flock to this event to savor the region's world-class wines while enjoying delectable local cuisine. With winery tours, tastings, live music, and culinary experiences, this festival is a perfect blend of relaxation and indulgence.

8. Adelaide Cabaret Festival:
For lovers of music, theater, and storytelling, the Adelaide Cabaret Festival offers a unique and intimate experience. Held over two weeks in June, this festival showcases local and international cabaret artists in various venues across Adelaide. From classic cabaret performances to innovative contemporary acts, this festival is a celebration of talent and creativity.

9. OzAsia Festival:
Dedicated to celebrating the diverse cultures of Asia, the OzAsia Festival is a captivating event that showcases contemporary arts, dance, music, and film. This festival provides a platform for
both established and emerging Asian artists, fostering cultural exchange and artistic collaboration. With mesmerizing performances

and immersive experiences, the OzAsia Festival offers a glimpse into the vibrant tapestry of Asia.

10. Adelaide Christmas Pageant:

Wrapping up the year with festive cheer, the Adelaide Christmas Pageant is a beloved tradition that delights both young and old. Held in November, this iconic parade features colorful floats, marching bands, clowns, and Santa Claus himself, heralding the arrival of the holiday season in Adelaide.

Adelaide and South Australia offer a remarkable array of festivals and events that captivate visitors year-round. Whether you're an art aficionado, a food and wine lover, or a music enthusiast, there is something for everyone in this vibrant region. The festivals and events mentioned in this travel guide are just a glimpse of the rich tapestry of experiences that await you in Adelaide and South Australia. Embark on a journey of cultural immersion and indulge in the warm hospitality of this enchanting part of Australia.

CHAPTER NINE

Exploring the Outback

•*Overview of the Australian Outback*

The Australian Outback, also known as the "Red Centre," is a vast and mesmerizing region that covers the majority of Australia's interior. Spanning over 2.5 million square miles, this arid and remote expanse offers a unique and captivating experience for adventurous travelers. From its ancient landscapes and fascinating wildlife to its rich cultural heritage and vibrant Aboriginal history, the Australian Outback is a destination like no other. In this comprehensive travel guide, we will delve into the highlights, attractions, activities, and practicalities of exploring this remarkable region.

Geography and Climate:

The Australian Outback is characterized by its arid and semi-arid landscapes, dominated by expansive deserts, rocky ranges, and stunning gorges. The most famous desert is the Great Sandy Desert in Western Australia, followed by the Gibson Desert and the Simpson Desert. The Outback is also home to the iconic Uluru (Ayers Rock) and Kata Tjuta (the Olgas), which hold deep cultural significance for the local Indigenous people.

The climate in the Outback is generally hot and dry, with scorching temperatures during the summer months (December to February) often exceeding 40°C (104°F). Winters (June to August) are more moderate, with pleasant daytime temperatures and cooler nights. It's essential to plan your visit accordingly, considering the weather conditions and the activities you wish to undertake.

Key Destinations and Attractions:

1. Uluru-Kata Tjuta National Park: This UNESCO World Heritage site showcases the iconic red monolith of Uluru, a sacred Aboriginal site. Nearby, Kata Tjuta offers stunning rock formations and beautiful hiking trails.

2. Kings Canyon: Located in Watarrka National Park, Kings Canyon features towering sandstone cliffs, breathtaking views, and the opportunity to undertake the challenging Rim Walk.

3. Kakadu National Park: A vast wilderness in the Northern Territory, Kakadu is renowned for its diverse wildlife, ancient rock art, dramatic waterfalls, and wetlands teeming with birdlife.

4. Alice Springs: Known as the gateway to the Outback, Alice Springs offers a blend of Aboriginal culture, historical landmarks, and stunning landscapes. Don't miss the chance to visit the Royal Flying Doctor Service and the School of the Air.

5. Coober Pedy: This unique opal mining town is located in South Australia and is famous for its underground houses, museums, and breathtaking opal mines.

6. The Kimberley: A remote and rugged region in Western Australia, the Kimberley is home to majestic gorges, pristine coastline, towering waterfalls, and a rich Indigenous heritage.

Activities and Experiences:
1. Aboriginal Cultural Experiences: Immerse yourself in the rich Indigenous culture of the Outback by participating in guided tours,

cultural performances, and visiting Aboriginal art centers.

2. Outback Wildlife Encounters: Spot kangaroos, emus, dingoes, and unique bird species as you explore the vast wilderness. Take a wildlife tour or embark on a self-guided adventure.

3. Outback Road Trips: Embark on an epic road trip through the Outback, experiencing the vastness of the landscapes, camping under starry skies, and visiting remote towns and attractions.

4. Hiking and Trekking: Lace up your boots and explore the numerous walking trails, such as the Larapinta Trail in the West MacDonnell Ranges or the Jatbula Trail in Nitmiluk National Park.

5. Camel Safaris: Enjoy a unique perspective of the Outback on a camel safari, traversing the desert landscapes and learning about the role of camels in Australian history.

Practicalities:
1. Safety and Precautions: The Australian Outback can be an unforgiving environment, so

it's crucial to be well-prepared. Carry ample water, sun protection, and a reliable GPS or map. Inform others of your travel plans and ensure you have appropriate travel insurance.

2. Accessibility: The Outback is vast, and some regions are remote and require careful planning. Consider the distances, fuel availability, and road conditions when planning your itinerary. It is recommended to rent a sturdy 4WD vehicle for the best experience.

3. Permits and Regulations: Some areas, such as national parks and Aboriginal lands, may require permits or have specific regulations. Research and obtain the necessary permits well in advance of your trip.

4. Accommodation: Options range from camping grounds and caravan parks to luxury resorts and remote eco-lodges. Plan your accommodations based on the region you're visiting and the level of comfort you desire.

Venturing into the Australian Outback is a remarkable journey into the heart of this vast continent. Its rugged beauty, rich cultural heritage, and unique wildlife make it an unparalleled destination for intrepid travelers. Whether you seek adventure, cultural immersion, or the chance to connect with nature, the Outback promises an experience that will leave an indelible mark on your travel memories. So, pack your sense of adventure, embrace the vastness, and embark on an unforgettable journey into the heart of Australia's Outback.

• *Uluru and Kata Tjuta*

Australia is a land of stunning natural wonders, and among them, Uluru and Kata Tjuta stand tall as two of the most iconic and awe-inspiring landmarks. Located in the heart of the Red Centre, these ancient rock formations hold deep cultural significance for the Aboriginal people and attract travelers from around the world. In this comprehensive travel guide, we will delve into the fascinating history, geological features, cultural importance, and the best ways to experience Uluru and Kata Tjuta.

I. Understanding Uluru:
A. Geographical and Geological Overview:

1. Location and Surroundings: Situated in Uluru-Kata Tjuta National Park in Australia's Northern Territory, Uluru is a massive sandstone monolith.

2. Formation and Composition: Learn about the unique geological processes that shaped Uluru, including its distinctive red coloration caused by iron oxide.

B. Cultural Significance:

1. Indigenous Heritage: Explore the deep connection between Uluru and the Anangu people, the traditional owners of the land.

2. Dreamtime Stories: Discover the rich mythology and spiritual beliefs associated with Uluru, as passed down through generations.

C. Must-Visit Sites and Activities:

1. Uluru Base Walk: Embark on a 10.6-kilometer trail encircling Uluru's base, offering breathtaking views and insights into its natural and cultural significance.

2. Talinguru Nyakunytjaku Viewing Area: Witness mesmerizing sunrises and sunsets that transform Uluru's color palette, capturing the essence of its beauty.

3. Field of Light: Experience the Field of Light art installation by Bruce Munro, where

thousands of illuminated stems create a mesmerizing visual display at dusk.

II. Exploring Kata Tjuta:

A. Introduction to Kata Tjuta:

1. Geological Features: Learn about the unique domed formations of Kata Tjuta, also known as the Olgas, and their distinct composition.

2. Cultural Significance: Understand the spiritual and cultural importance of Kata Tjuta to the Anangu people, who consider it sacred.

B. Key Attractions and Activities:

1. Walpa Gorge Walk: Embark on a 2.6-kilometer trek through Walpa Gorge, surrounded by towering rock walls, showcasing the area's unique flora and fauna.

2. Valley of the Winds Walk: Discover the captivating natural beauty of Kata Tjuta on this 7.4-kilometer trek, offering breathtaking views from various lookout points.

3. Sunset Viewing: Witness the remarkable transformation of Kata Tjuta's rock formations during the magical golden hour.

III. Practical Tips for Visiting Uluru and Kata Tjuta:

A. Best Time to Visit: Understand the climatic conditions and choose the ideal time to explore

Uluru and Kata Tjuta, considering factors such as weather, crowd levels, and events.

B. Accommodation and Facilities:
1. Ayers Rock Resort: Discover various accommodation options available, from luxury hotels to campsites, all offering easy access to Uluru and Kata Tjuta.
2. Cultural Centers: Visit the Cultural Centre to learn more about the local Aboriginal culture and gain a deeper understanding of Uluru and Kata Tjuta's significance.

C. Travel and Safety:
1. Getting There: Understand the transportation options, including flights, self-drive, and guided tours, to reach Uluru and Kata Tjuta.
2. Safety and Respect: Learn about important guidelines and cultural protocols to ensure a respectful visit to these sacred sites.

Uluru and Kata Tjuta are extraordinary natural landmarks that continue to captivate visitors with their timeless beauty and profound cultural significance. As you immerse yourself in the breathtaking landscapes, ancient stories, and vibrant traditions of the Anangu people, you'll create memories that will last a lifetime.

Make sure to plan your visit thoughtfully, respecting the cultural heritage of the region, and prepare to be awestruck by the majesty of Uluru and Kata Tjuta in the heart of Australia's Red Centre.

• *Alice Springs*

Nestled in the heart of the Australian Outback, Alice Springs is an enchanting town that serves as a gateway to the rugged and awe-inspiring landscapes of the Red Centre. Despite its remote location, Alice Springs is a vibrant and culturally rich destination that attracts travelers from around the world. With its unique blend of indigenous heritage, stunning natural wonders, and rich history, this iconic Australian town offers an unforgettable experience for those seeking adventure, cultural immersion, and a deeper connection to the land down under.

1. History and Indigenous Heritage:

Alice Springs has a rich history dating back tens of thousands of years, with the Arrernte Aboriginal people being the traditional custodians of the land. The town itself was established in 1872 as a telegraph repeater station, and it played a vital role in connecting

Australia with the rest of the world. Today, visitors can explore the Alice Springs Telegraph Station Historical Reserve, which offers insight into the region's early European settlement and the hardships faced by the pioneers.

2. Cultural Experiences:

One of the highlights of visiting Alice Springs is the opportunity to immerse oneself in the vibrant Aboriginal culture. The town is home to numerous art galleries, where visitors can admire and purchase authentic Aboriginal artworks. The Araluen Cultural Precinct is a must-visit, featuring the Araluen Arts Centre, which hosts exhibitions, performances, and workshops showcasing Aboriginal and Torres Strait Islander art and culture.

For a truly immersive experience, visitors can also participate in cultural tours led by local indigenous guides. These tours offer a unique perspective on the land, sharing ancient stories, traditional knowledge, and teaching visitors about bush tucker (bush food), traditional hunting techniques, and the significance of sacred sites.

3. Natural Wonders:

Alice Springs is surrounded by breathtaking natural wonders that will leave visitors in awe. The town sits at the gateway to the iconic Uluru-Kata Tjuta National Park, home to the world-famous Uluru (Ayers Rock) and Kata Tjuta (The Olgas). These sacred rock formations hold immense spiritual significance to the Anangu people and are a UNESCO World Heritage site. Witnessing the changing colors of Uluru at sunrise or sunset is a mesmerizing experience that should not be missed.

Another natural wonder near Alice Springs is the stunning Kings Canyon. This ancient sandstone formation features towering cliffs, lush valleys, and breathtaking views. The Rim Walk is a popular hiking trail that takes visitors on a 6-kilometer journey through the canyon, providing sweeping panoramas of the surrounding landscape.

4. Outdoor Adventures:
Alice Springs is a playground for outdoor enthusiasts, offering a wide range of activities to satisfy every adventurer. The West MacDonnell Ranges, known as Tjoritja by the local Arrernte people, stretch west of Alice Springs, showcasing spectacular gorges, hidden

waterholes, and picturesque swimming spots. Visitors can hike the famous Larapinta Trail, a 223-kilometer trek that winds through the ancient landscape, revealing stunning vistas at every turn.

For a unique and exhilarating experience, hot air ballooning over the Outback is a must-do. Drifting silently above the vast desert, watching the sunrise paint the landscape with golden hues, is an unforgettable moment that will be etched in your memory forever.

5. Festivals and Events:

Alice Springs comes alive with vibrant festivals and events that celebrate the diverse cultural tapestry of the region. The Alice Springs Beanie Festival, held annually in June, showcases the creativity of local artisans who create unique beanies (woollen hats). The event attracts visitors from far and wide and features workshops, competitions, and a market where visitors can purchase these handcrafted treasures.

The Camel Cup is another iconic event on the Alice Springs calendar. Taking place in July, this quirky race day brings together locals and visitors alike for a day of camel racing, live music, and family-friendly entertainment. It's an opportunity to witness the outback's unique sporting culture and enjoy a fun-filled day out in the sun.

Alice Springs, with its rich history, indigenous heritage, stunning natural wonders, and vibrant cultural scene, offers a unique and unforgettable experience for travelers seeking an authentic Australian outback adventure. Whether you're exploring ancient landscapes, engaging with the local Aboriginal culture, or embarking on thrilling outdoor activities, Alice Springs promises to leave an indelible mark on your journey through the land down under. So pack your bags, venture into the heart of Australia, and discover the magic of Alice Springs for yourself.

• *Outback Adventures*

Australia's outback is a vast and captivating region that holds an irresistible allure for adventure seekers and nature enthusiasts. With its rugged landscapes, rich cultural heritage, and unique wildlife, the Australian outback offers a once-in-a-lifetime experience for travelers. In this travel guide, we will delve into the wonders of the outback, highlighting its key attractions, activities, and practical tips to help you make the most of your journey.

1. *Discovering the Australian Outback:*
The Australian outback covers a significant portion of the country's interior, comprising arid deserts, stunning gorges, towering rock formations, and vast expanses of untouched wilderness. It spans across multiple states, including Western Australia, South Australia, Queensland, and the Northern Territory. Each region offers its own distinct charm and landscapes, providing endless opportunities for exploration.

2. *Key Destinations:*
a. Uluru-Kata Tjuta National Park: Located in the heart of Australia, this iconic destination is home to Uluru (Ayers Rock) and Kata Tjuta (the Olgas). Witness the mesmerizing sunrise and sunset over the majestic Uluru and embark on guided walks to learn about the area's spiritual and cultural significance.

b. Kakadu National Park: A UNESCO World Heritage site in the Northern Territory, Kakadu National Park showcases diverse ecosystems, ancient rock art, and abundant wildlife. Explore the park's wetlands, gorges, and waterfalls, and immerse yourself in Aboriginal culture.

c. Kimberley Region: Situated in Western Australia, the Kimberley is a remote and untouched wilderness known for its breathtaking landscapes. From the striking Bungle Bungle Range in Purnululu National Park to the dramatic Horizontal Falls in Talbot Bay, this region offers an unforgettable adventure.

d. Flinders Ranges: Located in South Australia, the Flinders Ranges is a rugged mountain range characterized by its stunning red rock formations, picturesque gorges, and rich Aboriginal history. Embark on bushwalks, 4WD expeditions, and witness the incredible wildlife, including emus and kangaroos.

3. Unforgettable Activities:
a. Camel Trekking: Experience the traditional mode of transport in the outback by embarking on a camel trek. Ride through the vast desert landscapes, camp under the stars, and learn about the history and role of camels in Australia's early exploration.

b. Outback Station Stays: Stay at a working cattle or sheep station to gain insights into the region's agricultural practices. Participate in mustering, horse riding, or sheep shearing, and enjoy the warm hospitality of the locals.

c. Aboriginal Cultural Experiences: Engage with the rich indigenous culture of the outback through guided tours and cultural activities. Learn about Dreamtime stories, witness traditional dances, and gain a deeper understanding of the land's spiritual significance.

d. 4WD Adventures: The outback is best explored by 4WD, allowing you to access remote areas and venture off the beaten track. Follow the Gibb River Road in the Kimberley, conquer the challenging Oodnadatta Track, or tackle the iconic Birdsville Track.

4. Practical Tips:

a. Weather and Climate: The outback's climate is characterized by extreme temperatures, with scorching summers and chilly winters. Be prepared for the conditions and pack appropriate clothing, sunscreen, and sufficient water supplies.

b. Safety Precautions: The outback can be unforgiving, so it's essential to take safety precautions. Inform others of your travel plans, carry a reliable GPS, and ensure your vehicle is in good condition. Additionally, be cautious of wildlife and avoid swimming in unfamiliar water bodies.

c. Travel Essentials: Stock up on essential supplies, including food, water, and fuel, as services can be limited in remote areas. It's also advisable to carry a comprehensive first-aid kit, insect repellent, and a satellite phone for emergencies.

d. Respect for Indigenous Culture: When visiting indigenous sites, it is crucial to respect local customs and traditions. Seek permission before entering sacred areas, refrain from taking photographs without consent, and follow any cultural protocols advised by local guides.

Embarking on an outback adventure in Australia is an awe-inspiring experience that promises to leave a lasting impression. From the iconic landmarks to the untouched wilderness and cultural encounters, the outback offers a diverse range of experiences that cater to all types of travelers. By immersing yourself in this enchanting landscape and respecting its natural and cultural heritage, you'll create cherished memories that will stay with you long after your journey concludes. So pack your bags, embark on a journey of discovery, and unlock the secrets of Australia's outback.

Camel Trekking

Australia's vast and awe-inspiring Outback is a destination that captures the imagination of adventure seekers from around the globe. Among the unique experiences it offers, camel trekking stands out as an extraordinary way to immerse yourself in the breathtaking landscapes and rich cultural heritage of this remote region. In this Australia travel guide, we will delve into the captivating world of camel trekking in the Australian Outback, highlighting the incredible journey it provides, the iconic sights to behold, and the cultural significance it holds for both locals and travelers.

1. History and Cultural Significance of Camel Trekking:

Camel trekking has a rich history in Australia, dating back to the mid-19th century when camels were imported from India and Afghanistan for use in exploration and transportation. These resilient animals played a crucial role in the development of outback regions, including the famous Ghan Railway construction. Today, camel trekking not only represents an adventurous activity but also pays homage to the pioneers who traversed this unforgiving terrain.

2. Choosing a Camel Trekking Adventure:

Several reputable tour operators in the Australian Outback offer camel trekking experiences, catering to different preferences and levels of adventure. Before embarking on your journey, it is essential to research and select a tour that suits your needs, considering factors such as the duration, difficulty level, accommodation options, and the itinerary's highlights. The most popular camel trekking destinations include Alice Springs, Uluru (Ayers Rock), and Broome.

3. *Highlights of a Camel Trekking Expedition:*

a) Majestic Landscapes: Camel trekking provides a unique vantage point to witness the awe-inspiring landscapes of the Australian Outback. As you traverse the vast deserts, including the Simpson Desert and the Great Victoria Desert, you will be treated to breathtaking views of sand dunes, rugged mountain ranges, and ancient rock formations.

b) Wildlife Encounters: The Outback is home to an array of unique wildlife, and camel trekking offers opportunities to observe these creatures in their natural habitat. Keep an eye out for kangaroos, emus, dingoes, and a variety of bird species, as your silent mode of transport allows you to get closer to the wildlife without causing disturbance.

c) Cultural Immersion: Interacting with the local Aboriginal communities during your camel trekking adventure provides a deeper understanding of the region's cultural heritage. Learn about ancient Dreamtime stories, bush survival skills, and the traditional uses of plants and wildlife.

d) Sunrise and Sunset Spectacles: The Outback is renowned for its captivating sunrises and sunsets, painting the sky with vibrant hues. Witness these breathtaking moments from the back of your camel, creating memories that will last a lifetime.

4. Practical Considerations and Essential Tips:

a) Fitness and Physical Preparation: Camel trekking requires a moderate level of physical fitness. Engaging in regular exercise and building endurance before your trip will enhance your enjoyment of the experience.

b) Packing Essentials: When embarking on a camel trek, pack light and bring essential items such as sunscreen, a hat, sunglasses, insect repellent, sturdy shoes, a reusable water bottle, and comfortable clothing suitable for both hot days and cool nights.

c) Respect for the Environment and Local Communities: The Outback is a delicate ecosystem, and it is essential to leave no trace of your presence during your camel trekking expedition. Follow the guidance of your guides and adhere to responsible tourism practices.

d) Weather Considerations: The Outback's weather can be extreme, with scorching temperatures during the day and cool nights. It is crucial to dress appropriately, stay hydrated, and be aware of any potential weather hazards.

Camel trekking in the Australian Outback presents a unique opportunity to disconnect from the modern world and immerse yourself in the rugged beauty of one of the world's most iconic landscapes. From traversing vast deserts to witnessing breathtaking sunrises and sunsets, this adventure offers an unforgettable experience that combines natural wonders, cultural encounters, and personal growth. So, embrace the spirit of the pioneers, saddle up on a camel, and embark on a remarkable journey through the heart of the Australian Outback.

Aboriginal Cultural Experiences

The Australian Outback, with its vast and rugged landscapes, holds a rich tapestry of history and culture. For thousands of years, Aboriginal peoples have called this land home, nurturing a deep connection with the natural environment and preserving their unique heritage. Today, travelers have the opportunity to engage with Aboriginal communities and partake in a range of cultural experiences that provide insight into their ancient traditions. In this travel guide, we will explore the Aboriginal cultural experiences available in the Australian Outback, offering an immersive and educational journey into the world's oldest living culture.

1. Understanding Aboriginal Culture:

To truly appreciate the Aboriginal cultural experiences in the Australian Outback, it is essential to gain a basic understanding of their culture, history, and traditions. Aboriginal peoples have a diverse range of languages, customs, and belief systems, each tied to their specific ancestral lands. Learning about the Dreamtime, creation stories, kinship systems, and art forms such as dot painting and storytelling will help visitors appreciate the depth and significance of their experiences.

2. Traditional Welcome Ceremonies:

Many Aboriginal communities offer traditional welcome ceremonies, known as "Welcome to Country" or "Acknowledgement of Country." These ceremonies involve a formal introduction to the land, traditional dances, music, and storytelling by the local Aboriginal custodians. It is a powerful way to begin an Aboriginal cultural journey, fostering a connection to the land and its original inhabitants.

3. Bush Walks and Cultural Tours:
Embarking on guided bush walks and cultural tours led by Aboriginal guides is an excellent way to gain a deeper understanding of the local environment and its cultural significance. Aboriginal guides share their knowledge of bush tucker (traditional food), medicinal plants, hunting techniques, and the spiritual significance of certain sites. These tours provide insights into the profound connection between the Aboriginal people and the land.

4. Rock Art and Cave Paintings:
The Australian Outback is adorned with ancient rock art and cave paintings, providing a glimpse into the Aboriginal people's rich history and cultural expression. Kakadu National Park, Uluru-Kata Tjuta National Park, and the Kimberley region are renowned for their rock art sites. Joining a guided tour or ranger-led walk to explore these sites ensures visitors receive accurate information while

respecting the cultural significance of these sacred places.

5. Cultural Festivals and Events:

Attending Aboriginal cultural festivals and events in the Outback allows visitors to witness the vibrant living culture firsthand. The Garma Festival in Arnhem Land, the Laura Dance Festival in Cape York, and the Tjungu Festival at Uluru are just a few examples of annual events that celebrate Aboriginal art, dance, music, and storytelling. These gatherings provide a unique opportunity to engage with Aboriginal communities, learn from their elders, and participate in cultural activities.

6. Aboriginal Art and Craft:

Aboriginal art is internationally renowned for its intricate designs, vibrant colors, and spiritual significance. Many Aboriginal communities have art centers where visitors can meet artists, watch them work, and purchase authentic artworks. These art centers often offer workshops where visitors can learn traditional painting techniques and create their own pieces under the guidance of skilled Aboriginal artists. Supporting Aboriginal artists and purchasing their artwork is an important way to contribute to the cultural preservation and economic sustainability of these communities.

7. Cultural Experiences in Remote Communities:

For a truly immersive Aboriginal cultural experience, consider visiting remote Aboriginal communities. These visits, often organized through responsible tour operators, offer a chance to connect with Aboriginal families, learn about their daily lives, and participate in cultural activities such as spear throwing, bush medicine workshops, and traditional dance performances. These interactions foster mutual understanding, respect, and appreciation of Aboriginal culture.

8. Aboriginal Culinary Experiences:

Exploring Aboriginal cuisine is an emerging trend
   in the culinary world. From bush tucker tastings to gourmet dining experiences incorporating native ingredients, visitors can savor the unique flavors of Aboriginal cuisine while learning about traditional food gathering and preparation methods. Guided food tours and cooking classes provide an opportunity to engage with local Aboriginal chefs and discover

the incredible diversity of Australian native ingredients.

Immersing oneself in Aboriginal cultural experiences in the Australian Outback is an enriching and enlightening journey. From traditional welcome ceremonies to exploring rock art sites, participating in cultural festivals, and connecting with remote Aboriginal communities, travelers have the opportunity to deepen their understanding and appreciation of the world's oldest living culture. These experiences not only provide insight into the past but also contribute to the cultural preservation and empowerment of Aboriginal communities. By engaging respectfully and responsibly, visitors can forge meaningful connections and leave with a renewed sense of the profound beauty and significance of Aboriginal culture in the Australian Outback.

National Parks and Natural Wonders

Title: Exploring Australia's Outback: National Parks and Natural Wonders

Introduction:

The vast and rugged Australian Outback is a treasure trove of natural wonders and national parks that captivate the imagination of adventurous travelers. From breathtaking rock formations to ancient landscapes, this vast region offers a unique opportunity to immerse oneself in the raw beauty and rich biodiversity of Australia. In this travel guide, we will delve into some of the most spectacular national parks and natural wonders that await you in the Australian Outback.

1. Uluru-Kata Tjuta National Park:
One of the most iconic landmarks in Australia, Uluru (Ayers Rock), is located in the heart of Uluru-Kata Tjuta National Park in the Northern Territory. This monolithic sandstone rock formation rises majestically from the desert floor, transforming hues of red and orange with the changing light. Visitors can embark on guided walks around the base of Uluru to learn about its cultural significance to the Anangu people. Nearby, Kata Tjuta (The Olgas) forms another striking formation, composed of 36 domed rock formations. The park offers visitors a glimpse into the ancient spiritual traditions and natural wonders of the region.

2. Kakadu National Park:
Situated in the Northern Territory, Kakadu National Park is a UNESCO World Heritage site renowned for its stunning landscapes and rich cultural heritage. This vast park covers an area of nearly 20,000 square kilometers and encompasses diverse ecosystems, including wetlands, woodlands, and sandstone escarpments. Visitors can explore ancient Aboriginal rock art sites, take boat cruises along the crocodile-filled waterways of Yellow Water Billabong, and witness the dramatic Jim Jim and Twin Falls. Kakadu National Park is a haven for wildlife, with over 280 bird species, saltwater crocodiles, and unique flora.

3. Purnululu National Park:
Nestled in Western Australia's Kimberley region, Purnululu National Park is home to the striking Bungle Bungle Range. These beehive-shaped rock formations are made of sandstone and feature vivid orange and black stripes, created by the contrasting lichens and algae. Visitors can explore the park's unique landscapes by taking guided walks, scenic flights, or 4WD tours. Cathedral Gorge and Echidna Chasm are two highlights, offering breathtaking views and a chance to witness the intricate beauty of the natural formations.

4. Flinders Ranges National Park:
Located in South Australia, the Flinders Ranges National Park is a magnificent landscape of rugged mountains, deep gorges, and expansive plains. This ancient region showcases a rich geological history spanning millions of years. Wilpena Pound, a natural amphitheater surrounded by towering peaks, is a must-visit. The park is also home to an array of wildlife, including kangaroos, emus, and wedge-tailed eagles. Visitors can explore the park through hiking trails, scenic drives, and Aboriginal cultural tours, immersing themselves in the region's unique history and natural beauty.

5. Karijini National Park:
Tucked away in the remote Pilbara region of Western Australia, Karijini National Park is a hidden gem. It boasts ancient gorges, cascading waterfalls, and tranquil rock pools, making it a paradise for nature enthusiasts. The park offers numerous hiking trails, allowing visitors to explore its captivating features such as Dales Gorge, Fortescue Falls, and Hancock Gorge. Adventurous travelers can also venture into the subterranean world of Weano Gorge and

witness the breathtaking beauty of Handrail Pool and Spider Walk.

Conclusion:
Title: Exploring Australia's Outback: National Parks and Natural Wonders

Introduction:
The vast and rugged Australian Outback is a treasure trove of natural wonders and national parks that captivate the imagination of adventurous travelers. From breathtaking rock formations to ancient landscapes, this vast region offers a unique opportunity to immerse oneself in the raw beauty and rich biodiversity of Australia. In this travel guide, we will delve into some of the most spectacular national parks and natural wonders that await you in the Australian Outback.

1. Uluru-Kata Tjuta National Park:
One of the most iconic landmarks in Australia, Uluru (Ayers Rock), is located in the heart of Uluru-Kata Tjuta National Park in the Northern Territory. This monolithic sandstone rock formation rises majestically from the desert floor, transforming hues of red and orange with the changing light. Visitors can embark on guided walks around the base of

Uluru to learn about its cultural significance to the Anangu people. Nearby, Kata Tjuta (The Olgas) forms another striking formation, composed of 36 domed rock formations. The park offers visitors a glimpse into the ancient spiritual traditions and natural wonders of the region.

2. Kakadu National Park:
Situated in the Northern Territory, Kakadu National Park is a UNESCO World Heritage site renowned for its stunning landscapes and rich cultural heritage. This vast park covers an area of nearly 20,000 square kilometers and encompasses diverse ecosystems, including wetlands, woodlands, and sandstone escarpments. Visitors can explore ancient Aboriginal rock art sites, take boat cruises along the crocodile-filled waterways of Yellow Water Billabong, and witness the dramatic Jim Jim and Twin Falls. Kakadu National Park is a haven for wildlife, with over 280 bird species, saltwater crocodiles, and unique flora.

3. Purnululu National Park:
Nestled in Western Australia's Kimberley region, Purnululu National Park is home to the striking Bungle Bungle Range. These beehive-shaped rock formations are made of

sandstone and feature vivid orange and black stripes, created by the contrasting lichens and algae. Visitors can explore the park's unique landscapes by taking guided walks, scenic flights, or 4WD tours. Cathedral Gorge and Echidna Chasm are two highlights, offering breathtaking views and a chance to witness the intricate beauty of the natural formations.

4. Flinders Ranges National Park:
Located in South Australia, the Flinders Ranges National Park is a magnificent landscape of rugged mountains, deep gorges, and expansive plains. This ancient region showcases a rich geological history spanning millions of years. Wilpena Pound, a natural amphitheater surrounded by towering peaks, is a must-visit. The park is also home to an array of wildlife, including kangaroos, emus, and wedge-tailed eagles. Visitors can explore the park through hiking trails, scenic drives, and Aboriginal cultural tours, immersing themselves in the region's unique history and natural beauty.

5. Karijini National Park:
Tucked away in the remote Pilbara region of Western Australia, Karijini National Park is a hidden gem. It boasts ancient gorges, cascading

waterfalls, and tranquil rock pools, making it a paradise for nature enthusiasts. The park offers numerous hiking trails, allowing visitors to explore its captivating features such as Dales Gorge, Fortescue Falls, and Hancock Gorge. Adventurous travelers can also venture into the subterranean world of Weano Gorge and witness the breathtaking beauty of Handrail Pool and Spider Walk.

Australia's Outback is a land of extraordinary beauty and diversity, encompassing national parks and natural wonders that are nothing short of awe-inspiring. From the iconic Uluru-Kata Tjuta National Park to the hidden marvels of Karijini National Park, each destination offers a unique experience and an opportunity to connect with nature on a profound level. As you embark on your Australian adventure, remember to respect the land and its traditional custodians, and immerse yourself in the rich cultural heritage that makes these natural wonders special.

CHAPTER TEN

Tasmania

•*Overview of Tasmania*

Located off the southeastern coast of mainland Australia, Tasmania is a captivating island state known for its pristine wilderness, diverse landscapes, and rich cultural heritage. With its untouched national parks, rugged mountains, beautiful beaches, and charming heritage towns, Tasmania offers a unique and unforgettable experience for travelers seeking an escape from the hustle and bustle of everyday life. In this Australia travel guide, we will delve into the wonders of Tasmania, exploring its natural beauty, wildlife, history, and must-visit destinations.

1. Geography and Climate:
Tasmania is the smallest state in Australia, covering an area of about 68,401 square

kilometers (26,410 square miles). The island is separated from mainland Australia by the Bass Strait. Its geography is diverse and includes mountains, rainforests, lakes, rivers, and stunning coastal areas. The climate in Tasmania is temperate, with cool summers and mild winters, making it an ideal year-round destination for outdoor activities.

2. Wildlife and Nature Reserves:

Tasmania is renowned for its unique flora and fauna, many of which are found nowhere else on Earth. The island is home to a range of wildlife, including the iconic Tasmanian devil, wombats, wallabies, pademelons, echidnas, and various bird species. Tasmania's national parks and nature reserves, such as Cradle Mountain-Lake St Clair National Park, Freycinet National Park, and Mount Field National Park, offer opportunities for hiking, camping, birdwatching, and wildlife spotting.

3. Hobart:

As the capital city of Tasmania, Hobart is a vibrant and charming destination that seamlessly blends history, culture, and natural beauty. The city's waterfront precinct, Salamanca Place, is a popular attraction, boasting sandstone warehouses converted into art galleries, cafes, restaurants, and boutiques. The iconic Salamanca Market, held every Saturday, is a must-visit for local produce, crafts, and live entertainment. Other notable attractions in Hobart include the historic Battery Point neighborhood, the Museum of Old and New Art (MONA), and the majestic Mount Wellington, offering panoramic views of the city and its surroundings.

4. Launceston and the Tamar Valley:

Located in northern Tasmania, Launceston is the state's second-largest city and offers a delightful mix of historical charm and natural beauty. The city's main attraction is Cataract Gorge, a stunning natural reserve with walking trails, a suspension bridge, and a chairlift offering panoramic views. The nearby Tamar Valley is renowned for its picturesque vineyards and wineries, where visitors can indulge in wine tasting and sample the region's finest produce.

5. East Coast:

Tasmania's East Coast is a pristine region known for its white sandy beaches, crystal-clear waters, and breathtaking coastal landscapes. The Bay of Fires, with its unique orange-hued rocks, is a highlight of this region and a haven for beach lovers and outdoor enthusiasts. Freycinet National Park is another must-visit destination, famous for Wineglass Bay, a secluded beach with turquoise waters and stunning views. Visitors can enjoy a range of activities, including hiking, kayaking, fishing, and exploring the region's charming coastal towns like Bicheno and Swansea.

6. West Coast and Wilderness:

The West Coast of Tasmania is a rugged and remote region characterized by untouched wilderness, ancient rainforests, and dramatic coastlines. Strahan, a historic port town, serves as a gateway to the UNESCO World Heritage-listed Franklin-Gordon Wild Rivers National Park. Here, visitors can embark on a cruise along the Gordon River, explore the dense rainforests, and witness the untouched beauty of this pristine wilderness.

7. History and Cultural Heritage:

Tasmania has a rich history that is deeply intertwined with its Aboriginal heritage, European settlement, and convict past. Port Arthur, a former penal colony, is a significant historical site and one of Australia's most important convict-era destinations. Visitors can take guided tours to learn about the hardships faced by the convicts and explore the well-preserved buildings and ruins. Other historical sites worth visiting include the Cascades Female Factory, Richmond Gaol, and the Queen Victoria Museum and Art Gallery in Launceston.

8. Food and Drink:
Tasmania has earned a reputation as a culinary hotspot, offering a diverse range of fresh produce, seafood, and award-winning cool-climate wines. The island is famous for its seafood, including Tasmanian salmon, oysters, and abalone. Visitors can explore the various farmers' markets, artisanal producers, and cellar doors scattered across the state, sampling local delights and indulging in farm-to-table dining experiences.

9. Outdoor Activities:
Tasmania's unspoiled natural landscapes provide endless opportunities for outdoor adventures. From hiking and bushwalking to mountain biking, kayaking, and wildlife cruises, the island caters to all levels of outdoor enthusiasts. The Overland Track, a multi-day hike through the World Heritage-listed Tasmanian Wilderness, is a bucket-list experience for avid hikers, while the Three

Capes Track offers breathtaking coastal vistas. For thrill-seekers, the Franklin River offers an exhilarating white-water rafting experience.

10. Festivals and Events:

Tasmania hosts a variety of festivals and events throughout the year, celebrating the island's unique culture, arts, and natural wonders. The Dark Mofo festival, held annually in Hobart, is a celebration of the winter solstice, featuring art installations, music performances, and unique culinary experiences. The Taste of Tasmania is a popular food and wine festival held over the New Year period, showcasing the best of Tasmania's culinary delights.

Tasmania offers a captivating blend of natural beauty, cultural heritage, and outdoor adventures. Whether you are seeking wilderness exploration, historical insights, or indulgent culinary experiences, this island state has something to offer every traveler. With its diverse landscapes, unique wildlife, and welcoming communities, Tasmania is a destination that will leave a lasting impression and create cherished memories for years to come.

• *Hobart*

Welcome to Hobart, the vibrant capital city of Tasmania, Australia's southernmost state. Nestled between the rugged beauty of Mount Wellington and the pristine waters of the River Derwent, Hobart offers a unique blend of natural wonders, rich history, and cultural attractions. This comprehensive travel guide will take you on a mesmerizing journey through Hobart, showcasing its breathtaking landscapes, fascinating heritage sites, culinary delights, and much more. Let's delve into the enchanting world of Hobart, where history meets contemporary charm.

1. Historical Significance and Cultural Heritage:

Hobart boasts a rich colonial past, and its historic sites are a testament to the city's heritage. Start your exploration at Battery Point, a charming neighborhood lined with well-preserved 19th-century cottages. Here, you'll find Arthur's Circus, a quaint square surrounded by Georgian buildings. Don't miss a visit to Salamanca Place, home to the famous Salamanca Market held every Saturday. This vibrant market showcases local artisans, food stalls, and live entertainment.

The iconic Constitution Dock, located on Hobart's waterfront, is a hub of maritime history and activity. It's the starting point for the renowned Sydney to Hobart Yacht Race, held annually on Boxing Day. Take a stroll along the historic Hunter Street, where you can discover unique boutiques, art galleries, and cafes.

2. Natural Wonders:

Hobart's natural beauty is awe-inspiring, with stunning landscapes and outdoor adventures awaiting you. Mount Wellington, standing tall at 1,271 meters, offers breathtaking panoramic views of the city and surrounding areas. You can hike or drive to the summit and enjoy the mesmerizing vistas.

For a closer encounter with nature, explore the nearby Mount Field National Park. Marvel at the majestic Russell Falls, go on a bushwalk through enchanting rainforests, or embark on a scenic drive through the park's diverse landscapes. Just a short ferry ride away, Bruny Island beckons with its pristine beaches, dramatic cliffs, and abundant wildlife, including fur seals and fairy penguins.

3. Art and Culture:

Hobart has a thriving arts scene, with numerous galleries and cultural institutions showcasing local and international talent. The Museum of Old and New Art (MONA) is a must-visit, housing an impressive collection of contemporary art and thought-provoking installations. Set within an underground labyrinth, MONA offers a truly unique and immersive experience.

The Tasmanian Museum and Art Gallery is another gem, featuring a diverse range of exhibits that delve into the state's natural and cultural heritage. The Theatre Royal, Australia's oldest continually operating theater, hosts an array of performances, including ballet, opera, and live theater shows.

4. Culinary Delights:

Hobart's culinary scene is a delightful fusion of fresh local produce, gourmet delights, and a thriving food and beverage culture. Start your gastronomic adventure at the Farm Gate Market, where you can sample the finest Tasmanian produce, from artisanal cheeses to organic fruits and vegetables. Indulge in a seafood feast at one of the waterfront restaurants, savoring the local delicacy, Tasmanian Atlantic salmon.

For a taste of Tasmania's vibrant wine industry, venture to the nearby Coal River Valley or Derwent Valley wine regions, renowned for their cool-climate wines. Take a tour of the vineyards, enjoy wine tastings, and pair your favorite drops with gourmet meals at the vineyard restaurants.

5. Festivals and Events:

Hobart hosts a vibrant calendar of festivals and events throughout the year, adding to its charm and cultural vibrancy. The Dark Mofo festival, held in winter, is a celebration of art, music, food, and light, with installations and performances transforming the city into a captivating wonderland. The Taste of Tasmania, held during the summer festive season, showcases the best of the state's food and beverages, accompanied by live entertainment and fireworks.

Hobart, with its captivating blend of history, natural beauty, artistic endeavors, and culinary delights, offers an unforgettable travel experience. From exploring historic neighborhoods to hiking through breathtaking landscapes, indulging in gourmet experiences to immersing yourself in art and culture,

Hobart has something to captivate every traveler. So pack your bags, venture to Australia's hidden gem, and let Hobart weave its magic on you.

• *Freycinet National Park*

Australia, a land of breathtaking landscapes, is renowned for its diverse and pristine national parks. Among these natural wonders lies the enchanting Freycinet National Park, a coastal sanctuary located on the stunning east coast of Tasmania. Spanning over 16,000 hectares, this remarkable park is a haven of untouched beauty, boasting stunning granite mountains, secluded white sandy beaches, crystal-clear turquoise waters, and abundant wildlife. In this comprehensive travel guide, we invite you to embark on an unforgettable journey through Freycinet National Park, discovering its captivating sights, engaging in thrilling activities, and immersing yourself in the sheer magnificence of this natural gem.

1. *Getting to Freycinet National Park*
To reach Freycinet National Park, travelers have multiple options. The closest major city is

Hobart, the capital of Tasmania, which is approximately a 2.5-hour drive away. Hobart offers domestic and international flights, making it an ideal starting point for your adventure. From Hobart, visitors can rent a car or join a guided tour to reach the park. Alternatively, Launceston, another major city in Tasmania, is approximately a 2-hour drive from Freycinet National Park, offering additional accessibility.

2. Climate and Best Time to Visit

Freycinet National Park experiences a cool temperate climate, with mild summers and cool winters. The best time to visit is during the summer months (December to February) when the weather is pleasant and ideal for outdoor activities. However, it's worth noting that this is the peak tourist season, so expect larger crowds. Spring (September to November) and autumn (March to May) also offer pleasant weather, and the park is relatively quieter during these seasons. Winter (June to August) brings cooler temperatures, but it can be a magical time to visit for those seeking tranquility and breathtaking scenery.

3. Key Attractions in Freycinet National Park

Freycinet National Park is renowned for its spectacular natural attractions, each offering a unique experience. Here are some must-visit highlights:

a) Wineglass Bay
Undoubtedly the crown jewel of the park, Wineglass Bay is an iconic destination that enchants visitors with its pristine white sands and azure waters. Accessible by a moderate hiking trail or via a scenic cruise, the bay offers breathtaking vistas from its lookout points and is a perfect spot for swimming, snorkeling, or simply basking in the beauty of nature.

b) Hazards Range
The Hazards Range, a series of striking pink granite peaks, dominates the landscape of Freycinet National Park. This rugged mountain range provides a stunning backdrop to the bay and offers various hiking trails catering to different skill levels. Whether you choose the shorter hikes to viewpoints or embark on a multi-day trek, the Hazards Range promises awe-inspiring panoramas and a chance to spot unique flora and fauna along the way.

c) Cape Tourville Lighthouse

Perched on a rocky headland, the Cape Tourville Lighthouse rewards visitors with panoramic vistas of the surrounding coastline, including dramatic cliffs and sparkling waters. A short walk leads to the lighthouse, and the nearby boardwalk offers a chance to observe the abundant birdlife and stunning seascapes.

d) Honeymoon Bay

Tucked away in a secluded cove, Honeymoon Bay is a picturesque haven known for its tranquil turquoise waters and pristine white sands. It's an idyllic spot for swimming, sunbathing, or enjoying a beach picnic while marveling at the surrounding natural beauty.

e) Sleepy Bay

Sleepy Bay, with its rocky outcrops and unique geological formations, is a haven for photographers and nature enthusiasts. Explore the coastal trails, breathe in the fresh sea air, and witness the dramatic clash of waves against the rocks as you soak in the serenity of this hidden gem.

4. Outdoor Activities and Adventure

Freycinet National Park offers an array of outdoor activities for adventure seekers. From thrilling hikes to water-based adventures, here are some exciting options:

a) Wineglass Bay Lookout and Hazards Beach Circuit

Embark on the iconic Wineglass Bay Lookout and Hazards Beach Circuit, a moderate to challenging full-day hike that showcases the best of the park's natural wonders. Traverse through lush forests, marvel at breathtaking vistas from Wineglass Bay Lookout, and descend to the secluded Hazards Beach for a refreshing dip in its crystal-clear waters.

b) Kayaking and Paddleboarding

Take to the pristine waters of Coles Bay and enjoy kayaking or paddleboarding amidst the coastal beauty. Whether you're a novice or experienced, these activities provide a unique perspective of the park's rugged coastline, secluded bays, and marine life.

c) Scenic Cruises

Embark on a scenic cruise around the peninsula, gliding along the turquoise waters and marveling at the towering granite peaks. These cruises offer opportunities for wildlife spotting, including dolphins, seals, and seabirds, and provide a relaxing way to soak in the park's breathtaking scenery.

d) Snorkeling and Diving

Discover the underwater wonders of Freycinet National Park through snorkeling or diving adventures. Immerse yourself in the vibrant marine ecosystem, encountering colorful fish, fascinating rock formations, and perhaps even encounter a friendly seal or two.

5. *Practical Information and Tips*

To ensure a smooth and memorable visit to Freycinet National Park, consider the following practical information and tips:

a) Accommodation Options

While there are no accommodations within the park, visitors can choose from a range of options in nearby towns such as Coles Bay and Swansea. These include campgrounds, holiday cabins, bed and breakfasts, and luxury lodges. It's advisable to book accommodation in advance, especially during peak season.

b) Park Entry and Passes

A valid National Parks Pass is required for entry to Freycinet National Park. Passes can be purchased online, at visitor centers, or self-registration stations at park entrances. It's essential to display the pass prominently on your vehicle's dashboard or carry it while hiking within the park.

c) Leave No Trace Principles
Respecting and preserving the park's pristine environment is crucial. Follow the Leave No Trace principles by disposing of waste responsibly, staying on designated trails, and refraining from feeding or approaching wildlife. Help protect the fragile ecosystems for future generations to enjoy.

d) Safety and Precautions
Be prepared for changeable weather conditions, carry sufficient water, and wear appropriate footwear and clothing for hiking. Check weather forecasts and trail conditions before setting out. Follow all safety signs and guidelines provided by the park authorities.

Freycinet National Park beckons travelers with its unparalleled natural beauty and abundant opportunities for adventure. Whether you seek tranquil moments on secluded beaches or exhilarating hikes with breathtaking views, this coastal sanctuary in Tasmania offers an unforgettable experience. Plan your visit wisely, immerse yourself in the magnificence of Wineglass Bay, explore the Hazards Range, and engage in thrilling activities amidst the unspoiled beauty of Freycinet National Park—an Australian treasure waiting to be discovered.

•*Cradle Mountain-Lake St. Clair National Park*

Located in the heart of Tasmania, Cradle Mountain-Lake St. Clair National Park is a breathtaking natural wonder that attracts nature enthusiasts from around the world. With its stunning alpine landscapes, ancient rainforests, and crystal-clear lakes, this national park offers a unique opportunity to immerse yourself in the raw beauty of Australia's wilderness. Spanning over 623 square kilometers, it is a UNESCO World Heritage site and a cherished part of the Tasmanian Wilderness World Heritage Area. In this comprehensive Australia travel guide, we will explore the magnificent features, activities, and practical information about Cradle Mountain-Lake St. Clair National Park.

1. Geographical Features

Cradle Mountain-Lake St. Clair National Park boasts a diverse range of geographical features that showcase the true splendor of Tasmania's wilderness. The park is anchored by two iconic landmarks: Cradle Mountain and Lake St. Clair.

a. Cradle Mountain: Towering at an impressive 1,545 meters, Cradle Mountain is a jagged dolerite peak that dominates the park's skyline. It offers a challenging yet rewarding hiking experience for outdoor enthusiasts. The surrounding glacial valleys, picturesque alpine meadows, and ancient rainforests provide a dramatic backdrop for nature lovers and photographers alike.

b. Lake St. Clair: Known as Australia's deepest lake, Lake St. Clair spans an impressive 200 meters at its deepest point. Surrounded by towering mountains and dense forests, this pristine lake offers tranquility and opportunities for water-based activities such as kayaking, fishing, and boating.

2. Flora and Fauna

Cradle Mountain-Lake St. Clair National Park is renowned for its rich biodiversity. The park is home to a vast array of unique plant species, including ancient rainforests, alpine heathlands, and button grass plains. The diversity of habitats supports a wide range of fauna, making it a haven for wildlife enthusiasts.

a. Wildlife: Visitors to the park may encounter iconic Australian animals such as wombats, pademelons, Tasmanian devils, and echidnas. Birdwatchers will delight in spotting native bird species like the colorful rosellas, currawongs, and the elusive wedge-tailed eagle.

b. Flora: The park showcases a remarkable variety of flora, including ancient species that have survived for thousands of years. Mosses, lichens, and ferns adorn the forest floors, while towering eucalyptus trees and pandani palms punctuate the landscape. The vibrant hues of wildflowers in the warmer months add a splash of color to the wilderness.

3. Outdoor Activities

Cradle Mountain-Lake St. Clair National Park offers a plethora of outdoor activities that cater to adventurers of all ages and abilities. Whether you seek thrilling experiences or a serene connection with nature, the park has something to offer everyone.

a. Hiking: The park features a network of well-maintained walking trails suitable for all levels of fitness. The iconic Overland Track, a 65-kilometer trek, takes you through stunning landscapes, including Cradle Mountain and Lake St. Clair. For shorter walks, options like the Dove Lake Circuit or Enchanted Walk offer picturesque scenery and captivating views.

b. Wildlife Spotting: Embark on wildlife spotting expeditions to catch a glimpse of the park's unique fauna. The dusk and dawn hours are particularly rewarding for encounters with wombats, wallabies, and Tasmanian devils.

c. Canoeing and Kayaking: Explore the pristine waters of Lake St. Clair by canoe or kayak. Paddle
along the shoreline, soak in the peaceful ambiance, and perhaps even spot a platypus or two.

d. Fishing: The park offers excellent opportunities for fishing enthusiasts. Cast your line in Lake St. Clair or the nearby rivers and streams, and try your luck at catching trout or salmon.

e. Photography: With its stunning landscapes, diverse wildlife, and ever-changing weather patterns, Cradle Mountain-Lake St. Clair National Park is a paradise for photographers. Capture the magic of sunrise or sunset over the mountains, or focus your lens on the intricate details of the park's unique flora and fauna.

4. Practical Information

a. Getting There: The park is located approximately 144 kilometers northwest of Hobart, Tasmania's capital city. It can be reached by car via the Cradle Link Road from Sheffield or by organized tours departing from Hobart or Launceston.

b. Accommodation: The park offers various accommodation options to suit different preferences and budgets. Visitors can choose from campgrounds, cabins, lodges, or nearby towns like Cradle Mountain Village.

c. Weather: Tasmania's weather is known for its unpredictability, so it is essential to be prepared for all conditions. Layered clothing, waterproof gear, sturdy footwear, and sun protection are recommended. Check the local weather forecast before your visit.

d. Park Entry: A National Parks Pass is required to enter Cradle Mountain-Lake St. Clair National Park. Passes can be purchased online or at the park's visitor centers.

e. Safety: While exploring the park, it is crucial to follow designated trails, stay alert for changing weather conditions, and adhere to wildlife safety guidelines. Be aware of any potential hazards, and consult park rangers for up-to-date information and advice.

Cradle Mountain-Lake St. Clair National Park offers an unrivaled opportunity to immerse yourself in the pristine beauty of Australia's wilderness. From the rugged grandeur of Cradle Mountain to the serene waters of Lake St. Clair, this national park provides an unforgettable experience for nature lovers, hikers, and outdoor enthusiasts. With its diverse flora and fauna, a range of outdoor activities, and stunning landscapes, Cradle Mountain-Lake St. Clair National Park is a must-visit destination for those seeking to connect with the raw beauty of Tasmania's wilderness.

• Historical Sites and Heritage

Welcome to Tasmania, Australia's island state, where history comes alive in the form of fascinating historical sites and heritage. This enchanting destination offers a unique blend of natural beauty and a rich cultural tapestry that dates back thousands of years. From ancient Aboriginal heritage to European settlement and the modern age, Tasmania's history is a captivating journey through time. In this comprehensive Australia travel guide, we invite you to discover the historical sites and heritage that make Tasmania a truly unforgettable destination.

1. Aboriginal Heritage:

Tasmania is home to an ancient culture that spans over 40,000 years. The Aboriginal people of Tasmania, known as the Palawa, have a deep connection to the land and a rich heritage that can be experienced through various historical sites. One such place is the Wukalina/Mount William National Park, jointly managed by the Tasmanian Aboriginal community and the Parks and Wildlife Service.

Here, visitors can participate in guided tours led by Palawa elders, learning about their history, traditions, and the significance of the landscape.

2. Port Arthur Historic Site:

One of the most iconic historical sites in Tasmania is the Port Arthur Historic Site, located on the Tasman Peninsula. This UNESCO World Heritage-listed site was once a notorious convict settlement during the 19th century. Today, it stands as a solemn reminder of Australia's convict past and offers a comprehensive insight into the hardships endured by convicts and the evolution of the penal system. The well-preserved buildings, gardens, and eerie ruins provide an immersive experience into Australia's colonial history.

3. Cascades Female Factory:

Located in Hobart, the Cascades Female Factory is another significant convict site with a focus on the experiences of female convicts. This site served as a punishment and reform institution for female prisoners, and visitors can take guided tours to understand the hardships faced by women during the convict era. The interpretive displays and personal stories shared by guides provide a poignant glimpse into the lives of these women and their struggle for survival.

4. Port Arthur Ghost Tour:

For the adventurous traveler seeking a spine-chilling experience, the Port Arthur Ghost Tour is a must-do. As the sun sets over the historic site, the atmosphere becomes charged with an eerie energy, making it an ideal time for a guided ghost tour. The experienced guides recount chilling tales of ghostly encounters and paranormal activities, adding a supernatural twist to Tasmania's history.

5. Tasmanian Museum and Art Gallery (TMAG):

In Hobart, the Tasmanian Museum and Art Gallery showcases a diverse collection of historical artifacts, artwork, and exhibits that delve into Tasmania's cultural and natural history. From Aboriginal artifacts to colonial-era displays and contemporary art, TMAG offers a comprehensive overview of the island's heritage.

6. Richmond Village:

Step back in time with a visit to Richmond Village, one of Tasmania's most charming and well-preserved historical towns. Just a short drive from Hobart, Richmond boasts an array of Georgian-style buildings, including Australia's oldest bridge, Richmond Bridge. Stroll through the quaint streets, visit historical sites like the Richmond Gaol, and immerse yourself in the colonial-era ambiance.

7. Beaconsfield Mine and Heritage Centre:

For a taste of Tasmania's mining history, head to the Beaconsfield Mine and Heritage Centre in northern Tasmania. This interactive museum showcases the region's rich mining heritage and pays tribute to the miners who toiled underground. The center offers underground mine tours, providing a glimpse into the challenging conditions faced by miners during the late 19th and early 20th centuries.

8. The Convict Trail:

Embark on an exploration of the Convict Trail, a network of historical sites and heritage buildings scattered across Tasmania

. This self-guided journey takes you through scenic landscapes and offers insights into the lives of convicts and the development of early settlements. Highlights along the trail include the Coal Mines Historic Site, Brickendon Estate, Woolmers Estate, and Ross Bridge.

9. *Low Head Pilot Station:*

Located near George Town, the Low Head Pilot Station is a historic complex that played a vital role in Tasmania's maritime history. Established in 1805, it served as a base for pilots who guided ships through the treacherous waters of Bass Strait. Today, the station houses a maritime museum, a lighthouse, and beautifully restored cottages that provide a glimpse into the lives of the early lighthouse keepers and their families.

Tasmania's historical sites and heritage offer an incredible opportunity to delve into the captivating stories of the island's past. From the ancient Aboriginal heritage to the remnants of the convict era and the development of colonial settlements, Tasmania's history is a tapestry woven with intrigue, resilience, and cultural diversity. Whether you're exploring the haunting ruins of Port Arthur, immersing yourself in the experiences of female convicts, or tracing the footsteps of early settlers along the Convict Trail, Tasmania promises an unforgettable journey through time. So, pack your bags and prepare to embark on a remarkable adventure that combines natural beauty with a deep appreciation for Tasmania's historical significance.

CHAPTER ELEVEN

Top Travel Tips

•Packing Essentials

Embarking on a journey to Australia promises breathtaking landscapes, unique wildlife, vibrant cities, and a rich cultural tapestry. To ensure a seamless and enjoyable experience, proper packing is crucial. This travel guide aims to provide you with an extensive list of packing essentials tailored to your Australian adventure. From clothing and footwear to travel documents and safety items, we've got you covered.

1. Travel Documents:

a. Passport: Ensure that your passport is valid for at least six months beyond your intended stay in Australia.

b. Visa: Check the specific visa requirements for your country and apply well in advance.

c. Itinerary: Keep a copy of your travel itinerary, including flight details, accommodation reservations, and any pre-booked activities.

2. Clothing:

a. Lightweight clothing: Pack breathable fabrics like cotton and linen to combat Australia's warm climate.

b. Layering options: Include a light jacket or cardigan for cooler evenings or visits to higher altitudes.

c. Swimwear: Australia's stunning beaches and coastal areas make swimwear a must-pack item.

d. Sun protection: Hats, sunglasses, and sunscreen with a high SPF are essential to shield yourself from Australia's intense sun.

e. Rain gear: A lightweight waterproof jacket or poncho will come in handy, especially during the rainy season.

3. Footwear:

a. Comfortable walking shoes: Australia offers numerous opportunities for outdoor exploration, so pack sturdy, comfortable shoes.

b. Sandals: Choose a pair of comfortable sandals for beach visits or casual strolls.

c. Hiking boots: If you plan to hike in national parks or explore rugged terrains, consider packing hiking boots with ankle support.

4. Electronics and Gadgets:

a. Power adapters: Australia uses Type I electrical outlets, so ensure you have the appropriate adapters for your devices.

b. Chargers and power banks: Keep your electronics powered up throughout your trip.

c. Camera: Capture the awe-inspiring landscapes and unique wildlife with a high-quality camera.

d. Portable Wi-Fi hotspot: Stay connected on the go by carrying a portable Wi-Fi hotspot or ensuring your mobile plan covers international data usage.

5. Health and Safety:

a. Travel insurance: Purchase comprehensive travel insurance to cover any unexpected medical expenses or trip disruptions.

b. Medications: If you take prescription medications, pack an adequate supply and carry them in their original packaging.

c. First aid kit: Include basic medical supplies like band-aids, antiseptic cream, pain relievers, and any personal medications or treatments.

d. Insect repellent: Australia is known for its diverse insect population, so carry an effective insect repellent.

e. Travel-sized hand sanitizer: Maintain good hygiene practices, especially when water and soap are not readily available.

6. Money and Communication:

a. Australian currency: Carry some Australian dollars for immediate expenses upon arrival.

b. Credit/debit cards: Ensure your cards are internationally accepted and inform your bank about your travel plans.

c. Mobile phone: Check if your phone is unlocked for international use or consider purchasing a local SIM card for cost-effective communication.

7. Miscellaneous:

a. Day backpack: Pack a lightweight, foldable day backpack for day trips and exploring cities.

b. Travel locks: Secure your belongings by using TSA-approved travel locks for luggage.

c. Travel guidebook and maps: Carry a reliable guidebook or download travel apps to navigate and discover Australia's hidden gems.

d. Reusable water bottle: Stay hydrated by carrying a reusable water bottle to refill throughout your journey.

Conclusion:
Australia's diverse landscapes and cultural experiences make it an enticing destination for travelers. By packing the essentials mentioned in this comprehensive guide, you'll be well-prepared to explore this beautiful country. Remember to research specific locations, weather conditions, and activities to further refine your packing list. With proper planning and packing, your trip to Australia is bound to be a memorable and fulfilling adventure.

• *Local Customs and Etiquette*

Australia, known for its breathtaking landscapes, vibrant cities, and diverse wildlife, is a country that welcomes millions of visitors each year. While it is essential to explore the country's attractions, it is equally important to familiarize yourself with the local customs and etiquette. Understanding and respecting Australian cultural norms will enhance your travel experience, foster positive interactions with locals, and ensure a memorable stay. In this comprehensive Australia travel guide, we delve into various aspects of local customs and etiquette, shedding light on social norms, greetings, dining etiquette, and more.

1. Greetings and Social Interactions:

In Australia, a friendly and casual attitude prevails, and people are generally warm and welcoming. Handshakes are the standard form of greeting, accompanied by direct eye contact and a genuine smile. Australians commonly address each other by their first names, even in formal settings, unless instructed otherwise. It is important to respect personal space and avoid physical contact unless invited. Additionally, Australians value punctuality and appreciate a phone call or text message if you're running late.

2. Cultural Diversity and Respect:

Australia is a culturally diverse nation, embracing people from various ethnic backgrounds. Respect for multiculturalism is deeply ingrained in Australian society. It is important to be open-minded, tolerant, and respectful towards people from different cultures, religions, and backgrounds. Avoid making generalizations or stereotypes, as Australians take pride in their multicultural heritage.

3. Australian Slang and Humor:

Australian English is often flavored with unique slang and idioms. While it may take some time to grasp the local lingo, understanding a few common terms can enhance your interactions. Australians have a penchant for humor, often utilizing sarcasm and self-deprecating jokes. Embrace the light-hearted banter, but be cautious not to offend anyone by crossing boundaries or making insensitive remarks.

4. Tipping and Service Culture:

Unlike some other countries, tipping is not a customary practice in Australia. The country has a strong minimum wage policy, and service charges are generally included in bills. However, if you receive exceptional service or feel inclined to show appreciation, a small tip or rounding up the bill is considered a polite gesture.

5. Dining Etiquette:

Australian dining culture is relaxed and informal. When invited to someone's home for a meal, it is customary to bring a small gift, such as a bottle of wine or a bouquet of flowers. Table manners are relatively casual, and it is acceptable to start eating as soon as you are served. When dining out, it is customary to wait to be seated and check if the restaurant has a self-service policy before ordering. Remember to say "please" and "thank you" to the staff, demonstrating your appreciation for their service.

6. Outdoor Culture and Sun Safety:

Australia is famous for its outdoor lifestyle, with beautiful beaches, national parks, and recreational activities. When engaging in outdoor activities, it is important to prioritize sun safety. Apply sunscreen regularly, wear a hat, and stay hydrated to protect yourself from the strong Australian sun. Respect environmental conservation efforts by avoiding littering and following designated trails in national parks.

7. Indigenous Culture and Protocols:

Australia's Indigenous cultures have a rich history that predates European settlement. When visiting areas with Indigenous significance, it is crucial to respect local customs and protocols. Seek permission before entering sacred sites, and avoid touching or removing any artifacts or natural resources. Participate in Indigenous cultural experiences responsibly, choosing operators that collaborate with local communities and adhere to ethical practices.

8. Sporting Culture:

Sports play a significant role in Australian culture, with cricket, Australian rules football, rugby, and soccer being popular. Australians are passionate about their sports teams and love engaging in friendly banter and debates.

If invited to watch a sporting event, embrace the lively atmosphere and cheer for the home team. Respect opposing fans and avoid any aggressive behavior or derogatory comments.

Understanding and embracing local customs and etiquette can greatly enrich your travel experience in Australia. By familiarizing yourself with Australian greetings, social norms, dining etiquette, and cultural diversity, you will be well-equipped to connect with locals and appreciate the country's vibrant culture. Remember to approach each interaction with an open mind, respect local customs, and enjoy the warm hospitality that Australia has to offer. Safe travels and have a memorable journey through the Land Down Under!

• Useful Phrases and Words

Planning a trip to Australia? Congratulations! With its stunning landscapes, unique wildlife, vibrant cities, and rich cultural heritage, Australia offers an unforgettable travel experience. To make the most of your journey, it's essential to familiarize yourself with some useful phrases and words commonly used in Australia. This comprehensive guide aims to equip you with the necessary language skills to navigate through the country and engage with locals effectively. Let's dive into the wonderful world of Australian English!

1. Greetings and Basic Expressions:

Australian English has its own set of colloquial greetings and expressions. Here are some essential ones:

- G'day: A typical Australian greeting, short for "Good day."
- How ya goin'?: A common way of asking how someone is doing.
- No worries: An iconic Australian phrase that means "It's okay" or "You're welcome."
- Cheers: Used to say thank you or goodbye.
- Ta: An abbreviation of "Thank you."

2. Ordering Food and Drinks:

Exploring Australia's diverse culinary scene is a must. Here are some phrases that will come in handy when dining out:

- Flat white/long black: Types of coffee commonly ordered in Australia.
- I'll have...: Start your order with this phrase when at a restaurant or café.
- Can I get the bill, please?: Requesting the bill at the end of your meal.
- Could I have some water, please?: Asking for water at a restaurant.
- What do you recommend?: Seek suggestions from the staff on their best dishes.

3. Getting Around:

Navigating Australia's vast landscapes and bustling cities requires effective communication. Here are some phrases for transportation:

- Where's the nearest bus stop/train station?: Asking for directions to public transportation.
- How much is a ticket to...?: Inquiring about ticket prices.
- Is this seat taken?: Asking if a seat is already occupied.

- Could you please tell me when we arrive at...?: Requesting assistance in being notified of your destination.

4. Accommodation:
Whether you're staying in a hotel, hostel, or Airbnb, these phrases will help you communicate with staff:

- Do you have any available rooms?: Inquiring about room availability.
- What time is check-in/check-out?: Asking about the designated times for checking in and out.
- Could you please bring me an extra towel/blanket?: Requesting additional amenities.
- Is breakfast included?: Verifying if your booking includes breakfast.

5. Shopping and Services:
Australia offers a fantastic shopping experience, and these phrases will assist you during your retail adventures:

- How much does this cost?: Asking about the price of an item.
- Do you have this in a different size/color?: Inquiring about alternative options.

- Could I try this on, please?: Requesting to try on clothing.
- Excuse me, where can I find...?: Asking for assistance in locating specific items.

6. Emergency Situations:

While we hope you won't encounter any emergencies, it's important to be prepared. Here are phrases for such situations:

- Call an ambulance/police!: Instructing someone to contact emergency services.
- I need help!: Seeking assistance urgently.
- Where is the nearest hospital/police station?: Asking for the location of essential services.
- My bag has been stolen!: Reporting a theft incident.

Equipping yourself with these essential phrases and words will enhance your travel experience in Australia. Remember, Australians are known for their friendliness and laid-back attitude, so don't be afraid to engage in conversations and immerse yourself in the local culture. Learning a few key phrases will not only facilitate communication but also help you create memorable connections with the people you meet along the way. Enjoy your journey through the diverse and captivating land of Australia!

•*Traveling with Kids*

Traveling with kids can be an exciting and rewarding experience, and Australia offers a plethora of family-friendly destinations and activities. From stunning beaches and national parks to vibrant cities and unique wildlife encounters, this travel guide will provide you with essential information and tips to ensure a memorable and enjoyable trip when exploring the land Down Under with your little ones. Whether you're planning a short getaway or an extended family vacation, Australia has something to offer for everyone.

I. Pre-Trip Planning:
1. Choosing the Right Destination:
   a. Sydney: Exploring the iconic Sydney Opera House, Taronga Zoo, and Bondi Beach.
   b. Melbourne: Discovering the Melbourne Museum, Melbourne Zoo, and Luna Park.
   c. Gold Coast: Enjoying the thrilling rides at theme parks like Dreamworld and Movie World.

d. Cairns: Embarking on a Great Barrier Reef adventure and exploring the Daintree Rainforest.

e. Perth: Visiting the Perth Zoo, Kings Park, and Cottesloe Beach.

2. Climate and Seasonal Considerations:
   a. Australia's seasons and weather patterns.
   b. Planning activities according to the climate.
   c. Packing appropriate clothing and essentials for varying weather conditions.

3. Accommodation Options:
   a. Family-friendly hotels and resorts.
   b. Vacation rentals and holiday homes.
   c. Caravan parks and camping grounds.

4. Health and Safety:
   a. Ensuring your kids' vaccinations are up to date.
   b. Safety tips for outdoor activities and natural environments.
   c. Car seat regulations and road safety.

II. Getting Around:
1. Domestic Flights:
   a. Major airlines and family-friendly policies.
   b. Booking tips and considerations.

c. Entertainment options for kids during the flight.

2. Ground Transportation:
   a. Renting a car and child safety seat guidelines.
   b. Public transportation options and accessibility.
   c. Booking tours and transfers.

III. Family-Friendly Activities:
1. Wildlife Encounters:
   a. Visiting zoos and wildlife sanctuaries.
   b. Kangaroo and koala encounters.
   c. Penguin parades on Phillip Island.

2. Beaches and Water Activities:
   a. Safe swimming beaches for kids.
   b. Surfing lessons and beachside activities.
   c. Snorkeling and swimming with dolphins.

3. Theme Parks and Amusement Centers:
   a. Exploring Australia's top theme parks.
   b. Thrilling rides and attractions for kids of all ages.
   c. Water parks and splash zones.

4. Museums and Interactive Exhibits:

a. Hands-on learning experiences for children.

b. Interactive science museums and art galleries.

c. Educational exhibits tailored for kids.

5. National Parks and Nature Reserves:

a. Exploring Australia's diverse landscapes and ecosystems.

b. Bushwalking trails suitable for families.

c. Wildlife spotting and camping adventures.

IV. Practical Tips for Traveling with Kids:

1. Packing Essentials:

a. Clothing, sun protection, and insect repellent.

b. Snacks, water bottles, and first aid kit.

c. Entertainment items for long journeys.

2. Maintaining Routines and Comfort:

a. Finding child-friendly restaurants and meal options.

b. Rest and nap times during the day.

c. Familiar toys and comforts from home.

3. Engaging Kids in the Journey:

a. Planning interactive and educational activities.

b. Involving children in decision-making.

c. Creating a travel journal or scrapbook.

4. Flexibility and Patience:

a. Allowing for downtime and relaxation.

b. Adapting to unexpected changes and challenges.

c. Embracing the spirit of adventure and discovery.

Traveling with kids in Australia can be a remarkable experience filled with lasting memories. By carefully planning your trip, considering your children's interests, and incorporating family-friendly activities, you can ensure a fun and enjoyable adventure for the whole family. From exploring iconic landmarks to immersing in Australia's stunning natural beauty, this travel guide has provided you with essential information and practical tips to embark on a successful journey across the enchanting landscapes of Australia with your little explorers.

• Staying Connected

Australia is a vast and diverse country known for its breathtaking landscapes, unique wildlife, and vibrant cities. When embarking on a journey to this beautiful land, staying connected is crucial for ensuring a smooth and enjoyable travel experience. From reliable mobile networks and internet connectivity to public Wi-Fi hotspots and communication options, this travel guide aims to provide you with essential information on how to stay connected during your visit to Australia.

1. Mobile Networks and Providers

Australia boasts a well-developed mobile network infrastructure that covers most populated areas, making it easy to stay connected on the go. The country operates on a tri-band GSM network, which is compatible with most international mobile phones. The major mobile network providers in Australia are Telstra, Optus, and Vodafone, offering extensive coverage across the country.

Telstra, known for its wide coverage, is often considered the most reliable network provider, particularly in remote areas. Optus and Vodafone also offer reliable coverage in urban areas and major tourist destinations. It is advisable to check coverage maps and compare plans and rates before choosing a provider that suits your needs.

2. SIM Cards and Prepaid Plans

To use your mobile phone in Australia, consider purchasing a local SIM card to take advantage of affordable local rates and data plans. SIM cards can be easily purchased at airports, convenience stores, or directly from mobile network provider stores. Ensure your phone is unlocked and compatible with Australian networks before purchasing a SIM card.

Prepaid plans are popular among travelers as they offer flexibility and control over expenses. Several providers offer prepaid SIM cards with data, call, and text allowances that can be recharged as needed. Compare plans from different providers to find the best value for your needs, considering factors such as data limits, call rates, and international roaming options.

3. Internet Connectivity

Australia provides reliable internet connectivity options, allowing travelers to stay connected and share their experiences online. Most hotels, cafes, and public places offer Wi-Fi access, although coverage and speed may vary. In major cities, you will find numerous internet cafes where you can use their computers or connect your own devices for a fee.

For more extended stays or remote areas, portable Wi-Fi devices, known as pocket Wi-Fi or MiFi, are convenient options. These devices allow you to connect multiple devices to a personal Wi-Fi network, providing internet access wherever there is cellular coverage. They can be rented from various providers or purchased outright if you plan to visit Australia regularly.

4. Public Wi-Fi Hotspots
Public Wi-Fi hotspots are widely available in Australia, particularly in major cities and tourist destinations. Many restaurants, shopping centers, libraries, and transportation hubs offer free Wi-Fi access to their patrons. However, it's important to exercise caution when using public Wi-Fi networks, as they may not always be secure. Avoid accessing sensitive information or making financial transactions on public networks unless you are using a trusted virtual private network (VPN) for added security.

5. Communication Options

In addition to mobile networks and internet connectivity, Australia offers various communication options for staying connected with family and friends. International calling cards can be purchased from convenience stores and supermarkets, allowing you to make international calls at affordable rates.

Messaging and calling apps such as WhatsApp, Skype, and FaceTime are popular alternatives for staying in touch with loved ones. These apps use internet connectivity and can help reduce communication costs, especially for international calls and texts.

Staying connected is essential for an enriching travel experience in Australia. With its reliable mobile networks, affordable prepaid plans, and widespread Wi-Fi access, staying connected with family and friends or navigating your way through this vast country becomes convenient. Remember

to compare mobile network providers, consider prepaid SIM cards, and make use of public Wi-Fi hotspots while prioritizing your online security. By staying connected, you can make the most of your Australian adventure and capture lifelong memories along the way.

•Safety Precautions

Traveling to Australia offers a plethora of captivating experiences, ranging from vibrant cities to stunning natural landscapes. To make the most of your journey and ensure a safe and memorable trip, it is crucial to be aware of the safety precautions that should be followed. This comprehensive travel guide provides an overview of essential safety measures to consider while exploring Australia. Whether you're planning a city adventure, a coastal road trip, or a bushwalk in the wilderness, adhering to these precautions will help safeguard your well-being throughout your Australian adventure.

1. General Safety Tips:

a. Research and Planning: Before embarking on your trip, gather information about your destinations, local customs, laws, and regulations. Stay updated on weather conditions, travel advisories, and any potential health risks.

b. Travel Insurance: Obtain comprehensive travel insurance that covers medical expenses, trip cancellation or interruption, and lost or stolen belongings.

c. Emergency Contacts: Keep a list of emergency contacts handy, including local emergency services, your embassy or consulate, and the contact details of your accommodation.

2. Health and Medical Precautions:

a. Vaccinations: Consult with your healthcare provider to ensure you are up-to-date on routine vaccinations and consider additional vaccines such as hepatitis A, typhoid, or influenza based on your travel plans.

b. Sun Protection: Australia experiences high levels of ultraviolet (UV) radiation. Protect yourself from sunburn and skin damage by wearing broad-spectrum sunscreen, a wide-brimmed hat, sunglasses, and lightweight protective clothing.

c. Water Safety: While the tap water is generally safe to drink in Australia, exercise caution when drinking from natural water sources in remote areas. If unsure, use water purification tablets or boil water before consumption.

d. Insect Precautions: Protect yourself against mosquito-borne illnesses, especially in tropical regions, by using insect repellent and wearing long-sleeved clothing during peak mosquito activity times.

e. Traveler's Medical Kit: Carry a well-stocked medical kit with essential items like pain relievers, antiseptics, bandages, and any necessary prescription medications.

3. Transportation Safety:

a. Road Safety: Familiarize yourself with Australian road rules and regulations. Always wear seat belts, obey speed limits, and avoid driving under the influence of alcohol or drugs. Stay alert for wildlife, which can pose hazards on rural roads.

b. Public Transport: Utilize reputable and licensed public transport services, such as buses, trains, and taxis. Keep an eye on your belongings, especially in crowded areas.

c. Car Rentals: Before renting a vehicle, carefully inspect it for any existing damage and ensure that it is roadworthy. Familiarize yourself with the local traffic rules and parking regulations.

4. Outdoor and Natural Hazards:

a. Beach Safety: Australian beaches can have strong currents and potentially dangerous marine life. Swim between the flags at patrolled beaches, heed warning signs, and follow lifeguard instructions. Do not swim alone, and be cautious of changing tides and powerful waves.

b. Bushfire Safety: Australia's summer months (December to February) bring an increased risk of bushfires. Stay informed about fire warnings, adhere to fire bans, and follow instructions from authorities. If camping, be mindful of fire safety and always extinguish flames properly.

c. Wildlife Encounters: Australia is known for its unique wildlife, including venomous snakes, spiders, and marine creatures. Educate yourself about potential hazards, maintain a safe distance, and avoid touching or provoking animals.

d. Hiking and Bushwalking: If planning outdoor activities, research your chosen trails, carry sufficient water, wear appropriate footwear and clothing, and inform someone of your plans. Consider the weather conditions and be prepared for sudden changes.

5. Personal Safety and Security:

a. Personal Belongings: Keep valuables and important documents secure, either in a hotel safe or on your person. Be cautious in crowded places and beware of pickpockets.

b. Personal Security: Stay aware of your surroundings and avoid walking alone late at night, particularly in unfamiliar areas. Use well-lit and populated routes when possible.

c. Scam Awareness: Be vigilant of common scams targeting tourists, such as fake tour operators, street games, and unofficial transportation services. Only use reputable and licensed operators.

d. Indigenous Cultural Respect: When visiting Aboriginal or Torres Strait Islander lands, respect local customs, sacred sites, and cultural protocols. Seek permission before photographing or recording indigenous people or their art.

Australia offers an incredible array of experiences, and by following these safety precautions, you can fully enjoy your adventure while minimizing potential risks. Remember to stay informed, plan ahead, and exercise caution in various situations. By prioritizing your safety and adhering to the guidelines outlined in this travel guide, you can have a wonderful and secure journey exploring the diverse wonders of Australia.

CHAPTER TWELVE

Conclusion

In conclusion, Australia is a captivating country that offers an endless array of experiences for travelers. From its breathtaking landscapes to its vibrant cities, Australia is a destination that truly has something for everyone. Throughout this travel guide, we have explored the diverse regions and highlighted the must-see attractions, cultural landmarks, and unique activities that make Australia an unforgettable place to visit.

One of the defining features of Australia is its stunning natural beauty. From the iconic Great Barrier Reef to the vast Outback, the country is home to some of the most awe-inspiring landscapes in the world. Whether you are exploring the ancient rock formations of Uluru, snorkeling among colorful coral reefs, or hiking through lush rainforests, Australia's natural wonders never fail to leave a lasting impression.

Beyond its natural attractions, Australia boasts a vibrant and cosmopolitan city culture.

Sydney, with its famous Opera House and Harbour Bridge, is a bustling metropolis that offers a mix of world-class dining, shopping, and entertainment options. Melbourne, known for its artsy laneways and vibrant café scene, is a city where creativity thrives. Other major cities like Brisbane, Adelaide, and Perth also have their own unique charms and are worth exploring.

Australia's rich Indigenous culture is an integral part of its identity, and visitors have the opportunity to learn about and appreciate this heritage. From visiting Aboriginal rock art sites in Kakadu National Park to participating in cultural tours and performances, experiencing Indigenous traditions can be a deeply enriching aspect of any trip to Australia.

For wildlife enthusiasts, Australia is a true paradise. The country is renowned for its diverse and unique animal species, many of which cannot be found anywhere else in the world. From cuddling koalas and hand-feeding kangaroos at wildlife sanctuaries to spotting whales off the coast or encountering crocodiles in the wild, there are countless opportunities to get up close and personal with Australia's incredible wildlife.

Australia is also a food and wine lover's paradise. The country's multicultural heritage has resulted in a vibrant culinary scene, with a wide range of international cuisines to explore. Whether you're indulging in fresh seafood by the beach, enjoying a gourmet meal in a top restaurant, or savoring local produce at farmers' markets, Australia offers a diverse and delicious food culture. Additionally, the country's renowned wine regions, such as the Barossa Valley and Margaret River, provide ample opportunities for wine tasting and vineyard tours.

Safety is a top priority when traveling, and Australia is generally considered a safe destination. However, it is still important to take necessary precautions and be aware of local laws and customs. It is advisable to have travel insurance and to stay informed about any travel advisories or warnings.

In terms of logistics, Australia has a well-developed transportation system, making it relatively easy to get around. Domestic flights connect major cities and regional areas, while an extensive network of highways and well-maintained roads allow for road trips and self-guided adventures. Public transportation options, such as trains and buses, are also available in most cities.

It's worth noting that Australia is a vast country, and it may not be possible to see everything in a single trip. It is important to plan and prioritize your itinerary based on your interests and the time available. Whether you choose to focus on a particular region or embark on a cross-country journey, Australia offers a wealth of experiences that will leave you with lifelong memories.

In conclusion, Australia is a destination that captures the imagination and leaves a lasting impression on travelers. With its stunning landscapes, vibrant cities, rich culture, unique wildlife, and culinary delights, it is a country that truly has it all. Whether you're seeking adventure, relaxation, cultural immersion, or a combination of all three, Australia offers endless possibilities. So pack your bags,embrace the spirit of adventure, and get ready to explore the wonders of Australia. Your journey awaits!